April de Ang

April   Angelis's plays include *Playhouse Creatures* (Sphi Theatre Company), *Hush* (Royal Court), *Soft Veng   e* (Graeae Theatre Company), *The Life and Time.   Fanny Hill* (adapted from the James Cleland novel   d *Ironmistress* (ReSisters Theatre Co.). Her work   radio includes *Visitants* (Radio 4) and *The Outl   er* (Radio 5), which won the Writers' Guild Awar   992), and, for opera, *Flight* with composer Jonath n Dove (Glyndebourne, 1998).

APRIL DE ANGELIS

Plays One

Ironmistress

Hush

Playhouse Creatures

The Positive Hour

Introduced by
the author

faber and faber

This collection first published in 1999
by Faber and Faber Limited
3 Queen Square London WC1N 3AU

Printed and bound
Antony Rowe Ltd,
Eastbourne, England

A CIP record for this book
is available from the British Library

ISBN 0–571–19709–4

To Ewan and Holly

Contents

Introduction

These four plays have been written over a period of ten years, which is as long as I've been working as a playwright. When I first started my main question was, 'How does anyone write anything longer than half an hour?' Having addressed that question other more devious ones arose. Maybe it's just me, but the strange thing about writing plays is that each time you come to do it you think, 'I don't know how to do this.'

While I was at university I had written a short play. From then on I was nagged by a feeling that I ought to write something. I thought everyone was nagged by that feeling so I took no notice. Then one day the nag changed its wording slightly to 'You won't be *happy* if you don't write something.' That was how I started.

Ironmistress was written in 1988 for Resisters, a women's theatre company that I had originally joined as an actress. When I was writing it I was trying to break away from the issue-based, 'agit-prop' style that a lot of theatre groups with strong political intentions had adopted for themselves. Writing in 1998, the failings of such a style seem glaringly obvious, but I can remember feeling daring as I tried to create something more theatrical. The other task I set myself was to write a woman character who was not sympathetic, who was perhaps as blameworthy as a patriarchal figure. (This also felt daring!) The reason *Ironmistress* is a two-hander is that that was all Resisters could afford. It was originally for reasons of economy that I gave Little Cog an alter ego; a way of getting three characters for the price of two.

Hush was a commission from the Royal Court Theatre.

It was produced in the theatre downstairs in 1992. This was my first experience of working with Max Stafford-Clark, whose rigorous approach to plays is invigorating. It made me really start to appreciate how much control a writer needs over their work. Max would never accept 'I don't know why that's there, I just like it.' He made me justify everything. With *Hush* I tried to write a play that an audience wouldn't necessarily attribute to a woman writer. I was attempting to address issues that didn't fit neatly under a feminist umbrella.

Playhouse Creatures began life as a commission from Sphinx Theatre Company and was first produced in 1993. Half-way through writing this play I had a baby. Because Sphinx had actually booked the tour before I had finished writing the play, I completed the last draft with my daughter in one arm and my pen in the other. That was my first intimation that motherhood and writing can be a tricky combination. The pleasure of writing this play was the opportunity to be absorbed in a fascinating historical period and to read about actresses – fascinating in any time. Out of the blue, a few years on, Dominic Dromgoole asked me if I thought it was possible to expand the play, originally written as a studio piece, to fit a bigger stage with the idea that it be included in the Peter Hall season of plays at the Old Vic. I said yes, but I was bluffing – I wasn't sure quite how to do it – but it never gets you anywhere to say no so I didn't. During rehearsals I rewrote the play further. I had the advantage of working with a great team, including the excellent Sheila Gish who was playing Mrs Betterton. 'Do we really need this bit?' she'd say with great tact and unerring accuracy. It is this version that is included here.

The Positive Hour was produced by Out of Joint (Max Stafford-Clark's company, formed after he left the Royal Court). Its starting point was my desire to look back and think, well, after twenty-five years of the women's movement, what? At the time I was writing it there was a lot of talk about 'laddism' (this already seems like an outmoded soundbite) and suddenly ground that had seemed well established in terms of feminism appeared to be being eroded. Women were 'babes' again, etc. But it was also true that there was a puritanical edge to some aspects of the feminism I had embraced back in the early eighties. Fifteen years later I wanted to look at that time more coolly. (Growing up? Growing conservative?) I hoped the tension between these ambivalences would resonate for an audience.

See what you think.

April De Angelis
July 1998

IRONMISTRESS

Characters

Martha Darby, *Ironmistress*
Little Cog, *her daughter*
(Shanny Pinns, *a fantasy*)

The date: 1840 or thereabouts

Ironmistress was commissioned and produced by the Resisters Theatre Company. It was first performed at the Young Vic Theatre Studio on 24 January 1989. It ran there for two weeks and then had a small London tour finishing at the Battersea Arts Centre for one week in April. The cast was as follows:

Martha Darby Gillian Brown
Little Cog Louise Waddington

Directed by Anna Birch
Designed by Caroline Burgess
Sound by Sylvia Hallet

Ironmistress had a second production with Blood and Honey Productions in summer 1989 and went to the Edinburgh Festival, then back to London again to the Man in the Moon Theatre.

Prologue

The sound of the furnace, of wind.
  Little Cog enters in the half-light.

Little Cog I can see everything from this hilltop.
Everything.
The chimneys of the iron-furnace, the roof of the iron
foundry.
I can hear things too, the hammer of the bellows
Pumping air to fan the furnace flames,
Or the cries of men
When hot metal is spat on their skin from the fires.

  Pause.

Do you know what they call this hill?
Deadman's hill.
They call it that because a dead man was found here once.
He was found right on this very spot.
I found him.
He didn't have a nose
Just a sort of hole
Where his nose would have been if he'd had one.
He'd been shot
In his face
And his arms were bent back in a funny way
Like he was dancing
And there was rusty blood, a lot,
All over his face and his neck and his chest.
He was dead.
Like the last dead man in a battle.
I didn't scream.

I hid in a bush instead and watched him for ages.
Then I went and picked up a twig
That was lying around
And stuck it into the bloody hole
Where his nose must have been, once.
I twiddled it round and around
A couple of times
To make sure he was really dead.
He was, because he never turned a hair.
Later I wished I'd never done it.
It's not religious to do that to the dead.
But then he'd been gone a long time.
He'd come back, you see, to the place
Where they made the bullet
That was put in the gun
That shot him.
Mr Soldier no-nose.

She laughs.

Silly old soldier.
Stupid ghost.
I can see everything from this hilltop.
The chimneys of the iron-furnace, the roof of the foundry.
Everything.

She exits.

*Lights up on Martha Darby who stands frozen and
statuelike. She is dressed circa nineteenth century.
    We watch her for a moment before she comes to life.
    She holds a small portrait in her hand.*

Martha What a handsome man!
Features made of granite.
It's me, Martha.
I'm not rubbing you out, I'm only dusting, darling.
You're not cross with me are you?

8

I do try to think of you every day, only . . .
There's so many things!
Sometimes I can't believe you're in a box in the ground,
That there's hardly anything left of you!
It doesn't seem possible.
Yesterday, I felt your breath on my neck,
But it was only the wind!
I shuddered . . .
Shuddered to think that ten years have passed.
How I miss you!
Your little ways . . .
You'd always use the same handkerchief for a month,
It would go stiff as an old leaf . . .
It's those sort of things that endear you to a person.
Time passes.
Clocks never show how much time is gone.
That's a failing.
Like never knowing how much money you've got in the
bank.

We hear faint singing.

Listen!
You know who that is!
Shhhh!
I'll surprise her.

She hides in the shadows.
    *The singing grows louder. It is Little Cog, Martha's
daughter. She sings the first few lines from the shadows.
As she enters we see she wears a white petticoat and
pantaloons.*

Little Cog Ye little insects who from open flowers
Extract your honey in the summer hours
Who learned you but the god omnipotent
He who made the stars and . . .

She hesitates . . .

Who learned you but the god omnipotent
He, who made the stars and . . . firmament!

She laughs . . . Martha interrupts from the darkness.

Martha Where did you learn a word like that?

Little Cog Why, Mother.
You gave me such a surprise!
I can feel my heart beating now.

Martha A word like that?

Little Cog Like what, Mother?

Martha has come out of the shadow.

Martha Like 'firmament'.

Little Cog Oh . . . that.
I . . . don't know.
I'm sure it just popped into my head.
God must have put it there.

Martha Did he?

Little Cog Yes, from the Bible.
The heavens and the firmament.
I'm sure now.
It wasn't from a science book.
I swear it.
They give me a frightful . . . headache.
And a cough.

She coughs.

Look, I've been learning a dance.

She demonstrates.

Pretty, isn't it?

She does a few more steps.

What does god look like?

Martha Only the dead know that. The good dead.

Little Cog I imagine he's all white, like a light
With a beard.
And he's wearing a sort of nightie.
Or . . .
Well, he'd have to wear something, wouldn't he?
He wouldn't go na . . .

Martha No.

Little Cog No.
Tell me a story
I've done my piano practice.
I don't know what to do.

Martha You know all the stories.

Little Cog Tell me again.
Tell me how I got my name.

Martha I've got things . . . to do.
Accounts.

Little Cog Addition, subtraction . . .

Martha Don't you worry about subtraction.

Little Cog Shall I show you my practising?

Martha No thank you.

Little Cog How I got my name then.

Pause.

Martha When you were . . .

Little Cog Yes, when I was born.

Martha When you were born . . .

Little Cog My father . . .

Martha Your father set his eyes upon you . . .

Little Cog He set them on me for the first time ever . . .

Martha And he said . . .

Little Cog And he said . . .

Martha You were . . .

Little Cog I was the sweetest . . .

Martha Like the smallest cog in a giant machine . . .

Little Cog The littlest cog in his machine!

Martha And the name . . .

Little Cog Just stuck!
Little Cog.

Pause.

Will you tell me another story now?
About Shanny Pinns.

Martha No.

Little Cog Ugly old Shanny Pinns.

Martha No.

Little Cog Ugly old evil Shanny Pinns who had a limp.

Martha Not that story.

Little Cog Who was so ugly you couldn't look at her you'd faint.

Martha Not that one.

Little Cog Old flaky skin.
Please.

Martha No!

Little Cog She'd scare children.
Shanny Pinns will get you!

Pause.

Why are you looking out of the window?

Martha I'm just looking.

Little Cog At the hill?

Martha The sun's gone in.

Pause.

Little Cog Do you know what day it is today?

Martha Today?

Little Cog You've forgotten.

Martha Of course I haven't forgotten.

Little Cog I knew you wouldn't.
I knew you wouldn't forget my last day.

Martha Your last day . . .
How wonderful.

Little Cog I can hardly believe it.
When I woke up this morning and looked at the sun I
thought 'I'll never look at it the same again'.
Things will be different.

Martha Yes.

Little Cog It's all happened so fast.

Martha Your dress is beautiful.

Little Cog Yes.

Martha White as a good soul.

Little Cog Or a ghost's arm.

Martha The bells will ring.

Little Cog They'll ring and ring and ring.

Martha You'll have a ring.

Little Cog And ring and ring.

Martha Everyone will be smiling.

Little Cog And ring and ring . . .

Martha You'll remember it for ever.

Little Cog And ring, ring and ring . . .

She stops suddenly.

Tell me.
Quickly.
What was yours like?

Martha Mine?
I've forgotten.

A pause. Little Cog looks at her.

Little Cog Tell me something else then.

Martha Don't you go on!

Little Cog Please.
Father . . . was he a great man?

Martha He was tall.

Little Cog Did you love him?

Martha And he liked riding.
He had a good seat . . . for a horse.

Martha fetches Little Cog's corset. They begin putting it on.

14

Little Cog We could play horses.

Martha Not today.

Little Cog All right.

Lays on the floor to facilitate matters.

Is the world a big place?

Martha Yes, quite large.

They move.

Little Cog Why did god bother to make other countries?

Martha After England he had a lot of time on his hands.

Little Cog He must have very big hands . . .

Martha So he made them for trading.

They move.

Little Cog What's that?

Martha Selling people things.

They move.

Little Cog What if people don't want them?

Martha They always do.
It's nature.

Little Cog Do donkeys want things?

Martha That's different.

Together they repeat the routine of movements which intersperses their dialogue.

Little Cog Do donkeys have kings and queens?
King donkey and gracious queen donkey?

Martha They're only beasts.

They move.

Little Cog And beautiful princess donkey
Which every donkey in the whole country wants her hoof
in marriage.

Martha They're not civilized, like us.
They don't understand the market.

Little Cog What's the market?

Martha It's where everything in the whole world is
bought and sold.
A perfect machine.
A free thing.

Martha gives an extra hard tug.

Little Cog Ooh, I feel dizzy.
My breath's gone somewhere.

They move.

Martha There!

She ties a knot.
    Little Cog moves, gingerly.

Little Cog Let's play horses!

Martha No, not horses.

Little Cog Horses!
I'm a giant horse
Called Alf.

Martha attempts to control her by 'reining her in'.
Little Cog snorts and stamps her foot.

Martha Not horses, Little Cog.

Little Cog Alf, the biggest horse in all the world.

Martha No.

Martha pulls at the laces, Little Cog gambols about.

Little Cog With the biggest feet.
She's enormous and very fast.

Martha No.

Little Cog Alf is a dark brown horse with teeth.
She can go anywhere.
Spain, anywhere.

Martha Not horses.

She has reined little Cog in.

Little Cog Why not horses?

Martha Because.

Little Cog Because?

Martha (*tearful*) You know it . . . upsets me.

Little Cog It makes you remember something.

Pause.

Martha (*faintly*) Yes . . .

Pause.

Little Cog Clip-clop, Clip-clop . . .

Martha He went riding . . .
It was a cold morning.
Wet hanging in the air.

Little Cog and Martha It had a bite.

Little Cog makes the sound of hoof beats.

Martha Wrap up warm!
I cried.

But you'd already gone
And were tiny in the distance.

Pause. We hear the beats.

At first when you got sick

Little Cog and Martha We thought nothing of it

Martha A cold

Little Cog and Martha It would surely pass.

Martha To help out I worked in the office for you
Neatly, efficiently
I could manage that you said

Little Cog and Martha With a sneeze.

They sneeze.

Martha I was glad of

Little Cog and Martha The task

Martha I had already learned that one can go

Little Cog and Martha MAD for nothing to do

Martha The cold moved to your chest
I restructured your filing system
You were pleased

Little Cog and Martha The cold gripped your lungs

Martha I finished your pamphlet concerning
The hot air blast you

Little Cog and Martha Were not so pleased.

Martha The cold took to you like

Little Cog and Martha Flame to paper.

Martha I met a deputation you

Little Cog and Martha Were not pleased at all

Martha I visited the furnace you turned your face to the wall and would not

Little Cog and Martha Speak then

Martha Life left you

The beats stop, they are still.

Little Cog Poor father.

Martha Poor Mr Darby.

Little Cog He died in this bed.

She lies on the floor.

Martha As requested, I buried him in an iron coffin

Little Cog Poor Daddy.

She begins to make his dying sounds . . . laboured breath.

Martha I didn't sleep all night.

Little Cog Poor Mummy.

Martha But then there was no one to tell me to come to bed.
I sat up.

Little Cog He's going . . .

Martha And read a book about cash-flow problems.

Little Cog Going . . .

Martha Night had never passed so fast.

Little Cog Gone.

Martha Next day it rained.

Little Cog Like tears.

Martha I sat looking out of the window
Like I'd never seen rain before!
I thought
In all this wet
Your iron coffin will sink deeper
Like a ship
In bad water.
Poor Abraham.

Little Cog Did you love him?

Martha (*lying*) Yes, of course I loved him.

Pause.

No new ironmaster.
Just me.

Little Cog And me.

Martha There was nothing else for it.
I had to do my duty.
A dreadful burden.

Little Cog Dreadful . . .

*Martha hangs her head. Little Cog steps back
respectfully, turns away. Pause.*
    Martha brings her head up suddenly.

Martha Letter to a man of business
From . . .
A woman of business!
Dear Sir,
Hello!

She stops, reconsiders . . .

No . . .
Dear Sir,
Life is . . . strange!

A short laugh.

Who knows along which path it may lead us?
We mortals.
It has fallen to my lot
(Tragically)
To become sole proprietress of the Darby Ironworks.
Once the property of the-late-Abraham-of-that-name-god-
rest-his-soul.
I pray to god for guidance.

Pause.

In fact I prayed to him concerning the little matter
Arising from your previous correspondence.
I have no power over inflation
That being in the hands of the almighty
And his market forces.
Sorry.

Pause.

I am forced to respond with an increase in the price
Of the raw materials I have on offer.
In other words if you want iron
For your locks and keys, sir,
You will have to pay for it.
I am not a charity.
Yours sincerely,
Martha.
PS. How is your dear wife?

Little Cog comes forward. She has a go herself . . .

Little Cog Letter to a man of business from a woman of
business!

She laughs.

Martha You know what happens to people who listen?

Little Cog No. What?

Martha Their ears.

Little Cog Their ears?

Martha Drop off. For eavesdropping.

Little Cog How horrible!

Martha Yes, messy.

Little Cog What do they do with them?

Martha Do?

Little Cog With their ears. When they've dropped off?

Martha Put them in a little box.

Little Cog Like a little coffin, for ears.

Martha picks up a ledger; she still has the pen. She begins to write.
The pen scratches. We hear the noise of the furnace . . . Little Cog seems to flinch at the sounds . . . They get louder . . .
Little Cog begins to talk over the sound of the furnace. They speak loudly.

Little Cog Is that the Bible?

Martha No.

Little Cog No it doesn't look like the Bible . . . You're writing in it.

Martha Yes.

Little Cog It's a book with numbers in.

Pause.

What sort of numbers?

Martha Not the sort you'd like.

Little Cog Oh.

Pause.

Let me see.

Martha No.

Little Cog Let me see.

Martha No.

Little Cog Let me.

Martha They're not good for you.

Little Cog Oh.

Pause.

Why can you look at the numbers?

*Pause. The noise is more insistent.
Little Cog moves suddenly.
Martha continues to write.*

Martha!
What's that you've got in your hand?

The noise fades. Martha stops.

Martha Nothing, Mother.

Little Cog Let me see.
Let me see.
Why it's a feather.
Why it's Father's quill pen.
His quill pen he uses for the accounts.
Where did you find that?
You've been where you shouldn't.
Where you shouldn't.
Creeping and sneaking.

Where you shouldn't.
What would Father say if he saw your hands so inky?
Let go.
Let go.
Now while I watch you.
Watch you.
What is the matter with you?
Let go.
Let go.

Martha Later I got back that feather pen
And swallowed it.
Hid it so no one else could have it
Or take it away.
I swallowed it like it was a piece of myself,
Better if it was iron, not feather.
I remember feeling cold even though it was a warm day.

> *Little Cog has been watching.*
> *Martha recovers herself . . . She looks at Little Cog.*

Remember that day!

> *She gets up . . . begins to hum a tune . . . she dances a few steps. She attempts to draw Little Cog in . . . slowly Little Cog gets drawn in.*

Little Cog There were so many people.
It was warm.

> *Martha continues to hum and dance.*

There's a man with an enormous . . . moustache!

Martha (*still dancing*) Business acquaintance.

Little Cog Business acquaintance!

> *Little Cog gets up and dances with Martha. They speak as they dance.*

24

Why does the woman he's with look unhappy?

Martha She's not unhappy.
She's his wife.
She's just being sensible.

They move apart, come together.

Little Cog I wouldn't want a husband with a moustache
like that.
It gets into everything.
Can't she make him shave it off?

Martha Shhh!

They move.

The first time I met the ironmasters he was there.
They were expecting ironmaster
Abraham . . .

They move, laugh.

Instead, there I was!
No one spoke for three minutes.

Little Cog And then?

Martha Someone got me a chair.

*Little Cog fetches a chair.
Martha sits.*

Little Cog And then?

Martha A glass of water.
A glass of water for the iron widow, they cried.

*The music becomes mock sad/melodrama. The style of
acting reflects this.*

Little Cog and Martha We'll help you, they chimed.

Martha Make you an offer you can't refuse.

Little Cog How poorly you look.

Martha I'll bear up, says I.

Little Cog and Martha Bear up, bear up, says they.

Little Cog Think of the figures, missus.

Martha Ah yes, the figures . . . I've trifled with them in the past. Long multiplication and the like.

Little Cog Iron's a damn dirty business, ma'am. Pardon me.

Little Cog and Martha Oooooh.

Martha collapses.

Little Cog The lady swoons!

Martha I'm merely adjusting my bootstrap, squire. In any case, I ablute regular.

Little Cog One needs iron in one's blood.

Martha I've never entertained anaemia, Master B.

Little Cog and Martha give a staccato laugh.

Little Cog A good offer, mind you. To take it off your hands.

Martha I leave my hands to god, sir. Him that made them.

They cross themselves.

Little Cog and Martha Amen.

Little Cog We'd leave you with the house.

Martha How kind, the house.

Little Cog Another sort of offer, widow. We're all good men.

Martha With wives! Sadly . . .

Little Cog Not ironmaster Dick. His wife was miserably seized of a malady of the foot. (*aside.*) She ran off.

Martha Yes, there is ironmaster Dick, asleep in his chair. He's worn well.

Little Cog Well, well.

Martha My own has so recently passed over . . .

Little Cog (*hopeful*) Yes, yes.

Martha I could not possibly entertain the thought. Before god.

Little Cog (*disappointed*) No, no.

Martha Farewell, gentlemen. Let's pray the price of furnace coke stays as cheap as the price of labour!

Little Cog and Martha dance a few more steps. It becomes more frenetic then suddenly stops.

Dance with someone else now, Little Cog.

Little Cog You said.
I said, 'I don't want to.'

Martha Dance with someone else.

Little Cog You said. I said, 'I want to dance with you.'

Martha With someone else.

She removes her hand from Little Cog's. She leaves Little Cog alone.

Little Cog You said.

Pause.

How lucky I did.
He wasn't how I'd expected.
He looked like an egg.

27

But apart from that he was very romantic.
I nearly fell asleep once though.
That's when he was talking about life in the frozen tundra.
It's an immensely fascinating subject.
He knew ever such a lot.
He talked about it too . . . a lot.
About how poverty in foreign countries had led them to
practise vices like not getting married and cannibalism.
But now we're selling them things like kettles
So it's all right.
And building railways
Miles and miles of iron track
So the kettles get there fast
and other things can come back.
He said.
When he looked at me he looked like an egg that was
hungry.
Is that possible?

Pause.

Why do some men go bald?

Martha They just do,
Some of them.

Little Cog We practised a lot after that, didn't we?

Little Cog leaves.
*Drawing-room music is heard; it has the suggestion
of the furnace in it.*
*Martha arranges two chairs side by side, facing the
audience. She puts them at a modest distance from each
other. She thinks, then puts them a little closer together.
She listens to the music.*

Martha You called this 'our song'.
I was very young.
We danced round and around.

28

I remember thinking, 'there's a hand on my back, perhaps
it won't ever go away'.
It's welded there.
I felt like I was high above everyone in the room.
Looking down,
Like a lost plaster angel.
Afterwards Mother told me it was because I was so happy.

She sits in one of the chairs and waits.
Little Cog enters, a bit too energetically.

Try again.

Little Cog enters again, more demurely. She sits. Her
petticoat sticks out. She pushes it down, awkwardly.
She looks sideways at Martha. She tries a smile. A
pause.

Little Cog I've been perusing a most fabulous book.

Pause.

Do you tamper with literature with any frequency Mr . . .
Mr . . . I can't remember his name!

Martha Just make up a name for now.

Little Cog looks round desperately. She sees an iron
dog.

Little Cog Mr . . . Dog!
Do you, Mr Dog?

Martha I've not much time for that sort of thing, Miss
Cog.

Little Cog Oh.

Pause.

The lady in it, Ismelda, is blown sideways off a cliff at a
most significant moment.

Pause.

I wept buckets.

Martha Don't say buckets.

Little Cog Teaspoons.

Martha Leave that bit out.

Little Cog thinks desperately. An idea strikes her.

Little Cog Have you been following the war, Mr Dog?

Martha Indubitably, Miss Cog.

Little Cog (*looking bemused, whispers*) What?

Martha (*whispers*) Yes, he's been following the war.

Little Cog What's indub . . . indubid . . .

Martha Just carry on. The war.

Pause.

Little Cog Do you know anyone who has died in the war, Mr Dog?

Martha looks at her worriedly.
Little Cog does not pick up the signal.

Or perhaps been fatally wounded?

Martha shakes her head.

Little Cog (*attempting a change of subject*) Mother says we're doing quite well because of the war.
There's a 'stimulation of demand'.
She's thrilled.

Little Cog catches Martha's eye.

She's . . . not thrilled . . .
But she's quite pleased!

She catches Martha's eye once more.

No . . . she's . . . she's . . .
I didn't mean to say pleased, I meant to say . . . to say . . .
feased!
Quite feased!
I just made a word up!

She laughs nervously.
Martha mouths something to Little Cog who follows
her stumblingly.

Oh . . . look at . . . look at me . . . I'm . . . bobbling? . . .
no, babbling! babbling on . . . you must . . . you must be
. . . must be . . .

She comprehends suddenly, claps her hands.

(*very fast*) Oh look at me I'm babbling on you must be in
need of some refreshment!

She looks pleased with herself.

Martha I'm fine thank you.

Pause.

Little Cog Oh.
But we ordered a cake.
It's very nice, with cream.
And small chocolate dots.
I wanted some.

Pause.

Why didn't he want any cake?

Martha He wasn't hungry.
Often, men don't eat cake.

Little Cog They don't?

Martha What next?

Little Cog I know.

She gets up. She sings.

My love went out upon a ship
The silver moon shone down
My love was a-coming to see me
But, alas, she drowned.
The waves grew high
Up to the sky
My love she lost her grip
Her poor white hands they loosed their hold
And she fell from the ship.
Oh cold cold waves
Cruel salty death
Her hair so fair, now sodden.
That is the path of tragedy
My love and I have trodden.

Martha applauds politely.

Why didn't she just hold on to some driftwood?

Martha signals for her to sit.

Why do I have to think of things to say all the time?
I'll never do it.
And I've got a spot.

Martha Try again.

Little Cog From the beginning.

Martha From the beginning.

Little Cog leaves . . . a thought strikes her . . . she returns.

Little Cog Close your eyes.

Martha My eyes?

Little Cog Your eyes.
Don't open them.

Martha closes her eyes.
  Little Cog puts on workboots and a shawl.

Martha What are you doing?

Little Cog Getting dressed.

Martha But it's not tomorrow yet!

Little Cog No.
I found some other clothes.

Martha Found them?

Little Cog Stand up, no looking.

Martha Found them?

Little Cog Come towards me.

Martha I'll fall!

Little Cog You won't. I'm watching.

Martha Where? Where did you find them?

Little Cog You look funny!

Martha I'll fall!

Little Cog Stop!

She spins Martha around.
  The sound of the furnace.

Martha Stop!

She spins her.

Stop!

Little Cog (*backing away*) Near the gates.
That's where I found them.

33

Martha The gates?

Little Cog Open your eyes.

Little Cog hides.
Martha looks.

Martha You're hiding.

Pause.

This is a game!

Little Cog appears in the shadows.

Little Cog Where are we?

Martha Ironstone house.

Little Cog No.
Outside.

Martha In the gardens.

Little Cog No.
Outside.

Martha (*quietly*) The hill . . .

Little Cog The very top.
Don't you know me?

Martha I haven't got time for this game.

Little Cog Don't you know me?

Martha Don't be silly.

Little Cog Me?
You do.

She gives a low moan.

Fuck.

She emerges from the shadow. In the workboots and

34

shawl she looks as though she is a different character.

I'm froze stiff as a slab.
Can't hardly feel nothing, my fingers, my feet, nothing.
Maybe I'm dead.
Thank god for that.
Jesus. Fuck.
I thought dead would be better than this
I might as well be alive at this rate.

Martha I don't know you.

Little Cog I went to sleep.
Next to a stinking great rock.
Pardon me, a rock.

Martha This is my hill.

Little Cog Very nice.
I fell asleep.
It was dark. I remember that much.
And cold.
Cold, as a bucket of ice.
Sometimes I get cold enough so I want to creep
Into the middle of the furnace.
Just drop down the top
Of one of its chimneys.
Then I'd burn up like a witch.

Martha Who are you?

Little Cog I work here.
Sorting, washing the ironstone.
You need that for iron.
The water's got lumps of ice in it now.
Your hands go bright red, like fire.
When they dry out they get cracks in them.

Last night I fell asleep where I sat.
Nothing they could do would move me.

I swore at them when they tried.

She laughs.

Trollops! Trulls! Drabs! Pieces! Mantraps!
You're foul-mouthed Shanny Pinns, they said.
You'll end up no good.
Too late for that, I said.
Then I was asleep.

Martha God would have got you home if you'd asked him properly.

Little Cog No he wouldn't.

Martha Yes he would.

Little Cog He wouldn't.

Martha He would.

Little Cog He wouldn't because I was lying.

Martha Lying!

Little Cog Yes, I always sleep out. I prefer it.

Martha You do?

Little Cog No.
I was lying again.
You believe anything, you do.
I live here.

Martha Here?

Little Cog Nowhere else.

Martha Shiftless!

Little Cog If you like.
I've got a confession.
To something bad.

Martha I don't want to hear it.

Little Cog It's a good one.

Martha It is?

Little Cog I've been somewhere.
Where I shouldn't.
Somewhere near.

Martha Near?

Little Cog Closer.

She moves closer.

Down there
Where it's hot.

Martha I'm sure I don't know what you mean.

Little Cog You do.
Down there.
Not on me.
Not the place you shouldn't touch yourself.

Martha I'm sure I don't know what you mean.

Little Cog (*laughs*) I mean past the place where the iron comes out
Like a hot red snake
Curling in the earth.
Past there.

Martha You've never been there.

Little Cog Have.
I stole up.

Martha Like a thief.

Little Cog I looked in, through the window.

She looks in through the window.

Martha A dirty-rag thief.

Little Cog Look.

Martha looks, cautious.

Martha Yes . . .

Little Cog It's smoky and exciting.
Like hell.

She laughs.

Martha You shouldn't have looked.
You should have prayed and thought about
Lot's wife.
Turned to salt.
For looking!

Little Cog Things in there.
Machines.
Metal, hot and twisted up.
Held in the fires.
Till it melts . . .
Melts . . .

Martha To salt!

Little Cog Then pulled,
Stretched and shaped.
Me, watching.
Till my head went in a spin!

Martha (*a little drawn in*) A spin . . .

Little Cog Hammers beating.
Making things . . .

Martha Yes . . .

Little Cog Bits for bridges.

Martha Yes . . .

Little Cog Linchpins.

Martha Yes . . .

Little Cog Links for a huge chain.

Martha I sell here dear what all the world desires, power!

Pause.

Somebody said to me . . . once . . . someone . . .

Little Cog I'm sick of the sight of stones.
Sick of cold.
I want to work in there.

Martha No.

Little Cog Why not?

Pause.

Martha Heat.

Little Cog Heat?

Martha Is bad.
Will arouse . . . things.
Hot, uncontrollable things.

Little Cog What sort of hot, uncontrollable things?

Martha Best you don't know.
A girl like you.
Sleeping on a hill.
Not in a house like everyone else.
You think you can just go there.
A place you shouldn't.
You're wrong.

Little Cog You go there. I've seen you.

Martha That's different. A duty.

Little Cog I want to work in there. With the machines
that go . . .

39

Martha Shush!

Little Cog I don't want to wash any more bloody stones.

Martha Good.
You're sacked.

Little Cog I'll starve.

Martha Not you, your sort.

Little Cog I'll be a ghost and come back and haunt you.

Martha Goodbye.

Little Cog Aren't you afraid?
Alone on the hill with me?
I could do anything.

Martha I'm not afraid.

Little Cog Maybe you should be.

Martha I've not got where I am today by being afraid.

Little Cog You hate me, I've made you remember
something and you hate me.

Martha I won't listen to another word.

Little Cog I'll do something.

Martha Something?

Little Cog I'll haunt you.

Martha Not another word.

Little Cog Haunt you!

> *Little Cog/Shanny backs away. We hear the sound of
> wind.*
> *Martha is left alone.*

Martha Ghosts are made of thin stuff, not metal.

They're nothing.
What can they do? Thinner than the wind!
I've always hated this hill.
Looming up out of the nice flat earth
Like the stomach of a woman swallowed in birth.
Like a breast nothing can suck dry.
I've not got where I am today . . .
I've not.
So many years I lay in a box.
Padded and quiet.
I had no key for it.
I lay in it like it was a stomach.
But I got out.
Oh yes.
Out.
Now the box and everything is mine.
They thought just because I'd been in a box
That I was as soft as its insides.
But I wasn't.
'Turn your back on me,
Turn your back on me, Mr Foreman
I pay your stinking wage, animal.
You're not good enough to lick the shit from my boot.
Next time you come in here.
To me.
You come on your knees or not at all.'
That was a battle. But he did it.
I sat on his back and rode him.
Like he was an animal too.

She laughs.

Christ, my hands felt like they were mine.
As we crawled over the morning-room carpet
I could hear the roar of the furnace
And the hammers beating in the foundry
The wind blowing on the hill of ironstone

Like they came from inside me.
And all that sweated, dirty life
shovelling coke,
beating hot iron
was like the workings of my own breath and body
So powerful.
And my mind!
Whoa, there, foreman!

She laughs.

I've had enough riding for today.

*She focuses on Little Cog, still hunched from the
previous scene. She no longer wears Shanny's clothes.*

There . . .
It's just a game gone strange . . .
Excitability . . .
That's all.
You found some clothes.
We'll burn them.

Little Cog No!
I'll burn them.
Later . . .

Pause.

(*to herself*) What shall I do now?
Next?
I know.
Something useful.

*She fetches paper and scissors. She begins to cut out
paper dolls.*

Doll, doll-doll, doll-doll-doll,
doll-doll-doll-doll, doll-doll-doll-doll-doll.

She holds them up.

These are my guests.
Look this guest is happy.
Because . . . she's happy.
This one's sad.
She's lost a son in the war.
A cannon splatted him.
This one's crying because it's a wedding.
This one's got a headache.
And this one's ugly and shouldn't be here.

She crumples up the dolls.

What time is it now?

Martha I don't know.

Little Cog The day's going.

Martha Yes.

Little Cog Soon it will be all gone.

Martha Yes.

Little Cog What shall I do now?

Martha Your sewing.

Little Cog I suppose so.
I've nearly finished my sampler.
I'm afraid to.

Martha Afraid?

Little Cog Because then I'll have to start another one.
Do you like sewing?

Martha (*lying*) Yes.

Little Cog Oh.

She gets up, walks over to the 'statue'.

She's very beautiful, isn't she?

43

Tell me about her again.

Martha You know the story, Little Cog.

Little Cog Tell me again.

She becomes the statue.

Father had her made.
In a giant mould.

Martha Cast her in iron.

Little Cog Nothing can hurt her now she's made of iron, can it?

Martha No.

Little Cog If she came alive, what would she do?

Martha Same as you.

Little Cog Sewing?

Martha Sewing.

Little Cog Oh.
She'd clank though, wouldn't she, while she sewed?

She makes the noise of the iron woman sewing.

Once I pressed my face to her iron chest.
I could have sworn I heard her heart beat.
A rattle like a tin bead.

Martha (*laughs*) Like she'd swallowed a tin bead.

A silence.

Little Cog Will I have lots to do, after?

Martha Yes.

Little Cog What?

Martha Things.

44

Little Cog Good.
Maybe I'll find a baby under a bush.

Lights down. Lights up on Martha alone.

Little Cog Spit it out Martha, spit it out.
Don't put things in your mouth and don't swallow them down.

Martha There's no other way to keep them safe.
Bits, things, pins, leg of a tin soldier, iron nibs.
Inside, mine.
Things disappear around the house.
A wedding ring, even.
I know where they lie.
Only me.
Mixed up in stomach juice.
What a dirty trick later.
Such a trick.
I knew she was coming from inside me.
I didn't know where from.
That was a shock.
They'd switched on some machine and not told me.
Still I've been good today.
Saw a spoon on the table
Didn't swallow it with my pudding.
It's weighing on me now though.
In the draw where anyone can get at it.
And me . . . empty.
I knew she was coming but I didn't know where from.
And Oh!
OH!
No, no.

Martha drops to her knees.

I didn't know where from.

Martha remains crouched on the floor.

45

Little Cog comes over to her and watches her.
She hesitates, tries a joke.

Little Cog Afternoon, Mr Dog. Mind if I smoke?

She laughs. Silence. She tries again.

One ironmaster says to another, 'My dog's got no nose'.
The other replies, 'How does it smell?'
The first says, 'Awful'.

Silence.

What are you doing?

Martha Looking for my keys.

Little Cog They're at your belt.

Martha So they are.
I thought for a moment I'd lost them.

She counts them.

The key to the foundry.
The key to the furnace.
The key to Ironstone House.

Little Cog They're at your belt.

Martha The first time I held them they felt . . . heavy.
I couldn't believe they were mine.
I even put them in my mouth . . . just to taste.
To see if they were real. Mine.
Felt like my bones had turned gold.
I'd never felt like that before.
Like a dream.

Little Cog Last night, I had a dream.
I'd grown as big as the world, nearly.
Me, Little Cog.
And I was iron

46

With iron bones.
My head was large as a huge nodding bell.
I rang terror.
My arms were bridges.
I was whirrs and clicks inside.
Then my beloved came.
I didn't see him . . . honest.
I was looking straight at the sun
Thinking I'd like to swallow it
Like a hot gold sweet.
Then I must have stumbled.
He cried out, 'My love'
Just as my knee
Pressed him to dust.
Making a cavern deep as an upside-down hill.
I couldn't even find a bit of his hair
For a locket.
I shouldn't have dreams like that, should I?

Martha He's very rich. He has a fine leg.

Little Cog The moon's come over the hill.
Let's light a candle.

They light a candle. The lights flicker.

When this candle's burned down it will be tomorrow.

Pause.

What's the percentage . . .

Martha Percentage?

Little Cog Possibility. What's the possibility of someone
. . . dying?

Martha Someone?

Little Cog No one in particular. Someone who'd just got
married, say.

47

Martha Don't be morbid. You're not going to die.

Little Cog I wasn't thinking of me.

Pause.

We could make a spell.
Would it work?

Martha No.

Little Cog Could it give someone a cold?
A serious one?

Martha Perhaps . . .

Little Cog Have you ever made one?

Martha No.
You couldn't trust a spell.

Pause.

Little Cog Oh!
I thought I saw the statue move.
But it was only the light.

Martha Of course it was the light.

Little Cog blows out the candle.

Little Cog!
You've blown out the candle.

Pause.

Where are you?
It's dark.

> *Little Cog puts on Shanny's clothes. She comes close to Martha. Martha jumps.*

Oh!

Little Cog This is the tale of how the iron statue was born.

48

A woman took off all her clothes.

She drops the shawl at her feet.

It was a cold night and she shivered.
The earth beneath her feet was muddy and soft.
She lay down in it.
Legs, stomach, rude bits.
She sunk into it like she was dead.
Hands helped from above, pushing her in.
Someone made a joke.
She couldn't hear the punch line though
Because by then her ears were mud-full.
When she had impressed herself
Well and truly
Into her pretend grave
They took her up and out of it.
Mud stuck to her like a shroud.
But at her feet
Was a deep earth shadow.
Into that they poured hot iron
Which quickly cooled
And was polished
They took such care of it,
Like lovers.
When the woman saw her iron double
She thought, 'Why have they given her such hard flesh?'
And 'Won't she get tired holding her arm up all the time?'
When she saw the iron face though,
Her breath stopped.
For it was the only face she'd ever seen
That said
Nothing.
She took her threepence and left.

She puts on the shawl.

Shanny Pinns knew that story because

She was the woman that lay
In the mud.
I swore I'd never do it again though
It was like looking at yourself, dead.
I only did it because I was hungry . . .

Martha One thing.

Little Cog Yes.

Martha No more stories.

Little Cog No more?

Martha They've gone with the night.

Little Cog But . . .

Martha Shhhh!
That's it.

>   *Pause.*
>   *Little Cog goes to take off the shawl. She changes her
>   mind and spins round like Shanny.*

Little Cog Trollops, trulls, drabs, pieces, mantraps . . .

>   *Martha grabs hold of her and forcibly stops her.*

Martha Stop it!

Little Cog Perhaps she's still in there.
They kept her inside,
An iron carcass.
A little thing inside,
Like something in a machine
That wants to get out.
A little Cog . . .
Little Cog!

Martha Stop it!
She's not here.

She's out on the hill.

Little Cog Yes.
In the wind!

Little Cog is held strongly by Martha. She tries to get free.

Martha What do you think she does on that hillside?

Little Cog Sleeps.
Lies in the grass.

Martha Yes she lies in the grass.
She doesn't get much sleep.

Little Cog She's not very tired. She's thinking of machine things.

Martha She's worn out.
People visit her.

Little Cog She likes that.

Martha Probably.
She would.
The men.

Little Cog (*stops*) The men?

Martha They come.

Little Cog They might, I suppose.

Martha Stinking of drink.

Little Cog (*laughs*) Pooh!

Martha She hears the change rattle in their pockets.

Little Cog They'd wake her up.

Martha She's not asleep.

Little Cog She hides.

Martha She says, 'Good evening'.
She drops her shawl.

Little Cog She'd get cold.

Martha She's burning up.

Little Cog She sings a song.

Martha It's done in silence.

Little Cog (*sings*) I'll go to the city to seek my fortune
I'll not wash stones any more . . .

Martha In the grass, which is wet.

Little Cog I'll go to the city 'tho I'm not pretty
I'll not wash stones any more . . .

Martha She's not expensive.

Little Cog Grey hard and lumpy, short not tall . . .

Martha A cheap sale.

Little Cog Once you've seen one stone you've seen them all . . .

Martha And quick. Quick.

Little Cog I feel funny.

Martha Then she lies in the grass and waits for the next.

Little Cog Funny, inside.

Martha She thinks of a cheap pair of gloves she will buy.

Little Cog Bad.

Martha Tarnished. Forget her.

Little Cog Forget her.
I feel bad.
I'm sorry.

Martha That's all right.

Little Cog I can't see her any more. In my head.

Martha Good.

Little Cog What's the thing she did in the grass?
Did she steal the money?
(*sings*) I'll not wash stones any more . . .
A cheap sale . . .

Martha Look at the dawn.

Little Cog Coming up over the hill.

Martha holds out her hand. Little Cog takes it.

My last day's over.

Martha Yes.
Come here.

Little Cog goes over to Martha. She lays her head in her lap. Pause.

Little Cog Is my hair an asset?

Martha If you take care of it.

Little Cog Oh but I do!

Pause.
Martha sings softly.
Pause.

Martha (*to Little Cog*) You're asleep.
The first time I heard him cough
I felt love.
A man with a weak chest.
The first thing I saw when I came here.
Was you,
An iron woman.

53

She indicates the statue.

I couldn't look at you.
I can't say why.
Then it got better.
I just never saw you.
Like you were made of glass or water
When was it?
Some night.
I couldn't sleep.
When I could hear the bellows at the furnace,
Hammering.
I could hear something else too.
I crept down to see.
Then I knew that really I hated you.
That was a shock.
Not because of what he was doing to you
But because you felt nothing.
And nothing could take seed.
Your expression never changed,
Not one flicker.
Of your iron lashes.
You knew nothing could take you, swallow you.

Afterwards,
As he stood leaning in your metal arms
Panting,
White, soft,
As he mopped you up with his night-cap.
I coughed,
Politely.
We never spoke after that,
Except at breakfast.
Perhaps that was how he caught his cold.
I hope so.
If one could be more forgetful.
Like a machine that remembers nothing.

Things would be simpler.
Remembered things are like spanners
Choking up the machine's pure workings.
Transactions should be
Grey and free of feeling,
Like iron.

We hear the noise of the furnace.

If one could be more forgetful . . .

*The noise gets louder. Lights fade. We hear church bells
mixed in with the noise of the furnace. The sound
fades. Lights up. Lights focus on Little Cog. She sits on
the floor tearing up her skirt.*
   *Martha enters. She wears a hat. She takes the hat off.
Little Cog ignores her.*

Your new home is lovely.

Pause. She ignores Little Cog's activities.

Thank you. I will sit down.

She sits down.

What are you doing?

Little Cog I'm making dolls.

Martha You're ruining your dress.

Little Cog Making them. Can't you see.
Look this one's happy because . . . she's happy.
This one's happy too . . .

Martha Ruining it.

Pause.

Little Cog Oh look at me, I'm babbling on you must be
in need of some refreshment.

Martha Tea would be pleasant.
A thirsty journey.

Little Cog Did you come through the gates, Mother?

Martha Of course I did, Little Cog.

Little Cog Did you notice?

Martha Notice?

Little Cog The gates are made of iron.

Martha And I drove through the splendid gardens.

Pause.

In full flower.

Pause.

This is a comfortable chair.

Little Cog I have important work to do, as you can see.
I've hardly a moment . . .
Hardly a moment . . .

She lets out a cry.

Martha What's the matter?

Little Cog A doll bit me.

Martha Bit you?

Little Cog No, I was lying.

Pause.

Martha This is a fine room.

Little Cog The bed was very white.
Someone had turned back the sheets.
I don't know who that was.

Martha Very . . . fine.

Little Cog He lay on top of me and made a sort of noise,
Ugh!
Like that.

Martha No.

Little Cog Yes.
He lay on me like I was something ugly he wanted to
squash.
I knew that because he had his eyes closed.
Then I felt him
His hands
Between my legs.
What's he doing that for, I thought?
I thought it was his hands
But I was wrong.
I tried a smile.
You know
The one we practised.
But of course as I said before his eyes were closed.
Then he started pushing me
Into me
Like I was a machine
He couldn't get started
A bad machine
Then I started to burn
Like I had hot metal inside me.
I couldn't find words
I was in a dark place
Amongst the furnace ash
Where things burn in the dark.
So I said nothing.
When it was finished
There was blood
Red
As melted iron
On my nightdress

Bright
Between my legs.
He seemed pleased at that.
I must have worked
Mustn't I?

Pause.

Martha I think I would like some tea now.

Little Cog Close your eyes.

Martha watches her as she puts on Shanny's clothes.

Martha You can't.

Little Cog hums and continues.

Not any more.
You can't because she starved on the hill.

Little Cog No, she didn't.

Martha She married then, and ate.

Little Cog No.

Martha Yes.
I've seen the parish records.

Little Cog No.
She nearly married, but not quite.

Martha Not quite?

Little Cog She got close.
Close enough so she could smell the priest
Then she surprised herself
And said 'no'.

Martha She died then.

Little Cog No.

Martha Sold herself, rotted and died of the pox.

Little Cog That's not the story.

Martha No, you're right.
I remember now, the day she met her end.

Little Cog The story is she still went to the foundry and
watched the machines.

Martha It was the day the crowd came.
Indistinguishable as a bag of old machine parts.

Little Cog She even made some machines up.

Martha The crowd smelled.

Little Cog Small ones, big ones.

Martha Like a dirty sea.
With dirty things awash in it.

Little Cog Machines for making food.

Martha Their cry was the crash of a dirty wave
On an old sea wall.

Little Cog She said being hungry was like living with a rat.

Martha They came close.

Little Cog A rat inside you that gnaws.

Martha Close up to Ironstone House.

Little Cog When you've got it, the rat.
You feel like a rat.

Martha Pressed close to its beautiful iron gates.

Little Cog Like you must be bad.

Martha Hard work is the way to plenty, I cried.

Little Cog It's the hardest thing to remember you're not.

Martha The harder you work the more wealth for everyone.

Little Cog Not bad.

Martha They had a red rag, like a flag, red from the blood of some animal.

Little Cog Then there was blood.

Martha Your distress rises from your own bad management!

Little Cog Bright between my legs.

Martha I can distribute recipes for a few cheap dishes amongst you . . .

Martha reacts with a small cry, as if something is flung at her face.

And then something threw muck at my face.
A woman, I think.
'Try feeding your daughters on that,' she cried.

Little Cog It stuck to your cheek, like blood.

Martha Pressing closer to the gates.

Little Cog You were frightened.
There was nothing you could do.

Martha Red Soldiers stood about.

Little Cog No!
They couldn't get there in time.

Martha They came over the hill like clockwork.

Little Cog They'd forgotten to load their guns!

Martha They were full as stomachs.

They speak the next two lines simultaneously.

Little Cog Empty!

Martha Fire!

Brief pause.

There was a moment's silence, like after a kiss.
Then the noise.
That's when I saw the woman fall.

Little Cog No!

Martha And it was her, Shanny Pinns.

Little Cog falls, clutching her stomach.

Little Cog (*whispers*) No . . .

She drops her head.

Martha Later the rest went back to work.

Pause.
Little Cog brings her head up.

Little Cog They missed.

Martha They didn't. I saw.

Little Cog They did.
A soldier shot himself by mistake.
That's what you saw.
She got away.

Pause.

Martha And then . . .?

Little Cog And then . . .

Martha What?

Little Cog She . . . she . . .

Martha Nothing.

There's nothing she could do.
She's a part that doesn't fit.
A ghost on a hill.

Little Cog I'm not listening!

Pause.

She . . .

Martha Yes?

Little Cog She became a highwayman!

Martha Impossible!

Little Cog She did.
She liked the outfit for a start.
Trousers and a hat.

Martha Unnatural.

Little Cog You were in your carriage.

Martha I never met her!

The sound of wind is heard. The lights have already changed . . . a dark, rainy night. A storm!

Little Cog You're just not remembering!
You're in your carriage
And the coachman says something to you
Only you can't hear him because of the wind . . .

Little Cog's voice fades . . . she retreats to the shadows.
    Martha is seated as if in a carriage.

Martha What's that you say, coachman?
This is a bad road?
That is merely peasant superstition.
My! How the wind howls
And the trees claw at the carriage top

62

As if they held a grudge against me.
But I have done nothing.
The horses fly faster
You beat them as if your very life depended on it.

*She laughs. There is a crash of thunder. Martha reacts
to the coach juddering, etc.*

Coachman!
Come back!
Use your whip, coward!
Or at least leave it here with me . . .

Little Cog jumps forward.

Little Cog Something leaps from the shadows.
You wonder if it has horns.
But it's her!
She laughs, evilly.

Little Cog laughs evilly.

And brandishes her shiny pistol which she built herself
from bits of this and that.

Martha What do you want?

Little Cog But she does not answer you.
There is only the sound of the wind instead.

We hear a burst of wind.

Then she takes the stones from your neck.

Martha touches her neck.

The rings from your fingers.

Martha clenches her fists.

And the purse from your pocket!
Then she laughs, vindictively.

Little Cog laughs vindictively.

And you say . . . you'll . . .

Martha You'll . . .

Little Cog Never

Martha Never

Little Cog Get

Martha Get

Little Cog Away

Martha You'll never get away with it!

Little Cog Then she laughs piratically.

Little Cog laughs piratically.

And slaps her thigh.

She does so.

Then they both stop dead.

They do so.

But it's only her fast horse, Alf,
Snorting and stamping in the forest.
I'll be gone from here in a ship, says she.
No one will ever find me.

Martha You'll swing!
That's the only breeze you'll feel, no sea breeze.

Little Cog She laughs challengingly.

She laughs challengingly.

I'm off to a foreign port
To set myself up as a maker of diverse machines.
Painless tooth-pulling machines,

64

Dog-walking machines,
Even a metal bird machine that flies in the sky
With people having a lift in it.

Martha Fancies!

Little Cog No.
She sets your horses loose.
Biting through the reins with her teeth
Jumps up on her faithful Alf
And thunders off into the distance . . .

Little Cog runs a few steps.

Wait!

Pause.

She's gone.

Pause.

Sometimes when I wake here in the mornings,
Just for that first moment,
I think I've been buried.

Martha I never did have tea, did I?

Pause.

Kiss me goodbye.

Little Cog doesn't move.

When I was a child I remember sitting on the grass.
I had no desire to swallow it.
I couldn't tell which was me and which was the grass!
I felt happy.
Stupidly.
Slowly, I learned though.
Learned that the whole world, you, me,
God, is a giant machine.

All separate bits,
That mustn't be tampered with.
And those of us who hold its life in our hands
Have only to act according to the dictates
Of our moral faculties
Thereby pursuing the most effective means
For promoting the happiness of mankind.
Kiss me goodbye.

> *Little Cog looks at her but does not approach.*

Little Cog Goodbye.

> *Lights fade slowly.*
> *The sound of the furnace; lights flicker red.*

Martha Alone.
I still have everything.

> *Pause.*

What happens when you die?
A slow disappearing act.
Face tissues fall off with a sigh.
Your one last expression
Holds out as long as it can
Before vanishing
To an insect's mouth.
Neck, knees, back-skin,
Wrist flesh,
All go.
You go.
Worse,
Everything that was ever yours
Isn't yours any more.
Not one thing.
Your hands can hold no more keys.
Swallowing is pointless.
There must be a way to stop this dreadful letting go . . .

This passing on!
I would take the whole world with me if I could.
Every blade of grass,
Every smile,
Every piece of food,
Every monument and house.
Everything.
It would make the biggest fire ever
And a wind.
The machine would stop.

Lights down fast. The sound fades.
Martha exits.
Little Cog enters as Shanny Pinns.

Shanny/Little Cog Wait!
That's not the story
So much time has passed.
A hundred years, more.
A girl walks on this hill,
She finds things, strange things.
A metal woman
Lying in the earth
With one arm stretched out
Clutching at the wind
Or asking for something.
The girl sat on her shoulder
And watched for birds.
She likes birds.
She wants to know how they work.
Sometimes she says to herself . . .
'I'll see the soldier if I'm not careful'
'I'll see the hole in his face and wish I'd stayed home.'
She thinks that dead or not the soldier may have a gun or
iron knife,
He may hold her arm and not let her go.
Then she feels like there's a bird in her chest

Beating its wings in a panic to get out
But really it's her heart.
I only come here for the birds, she thinks.
One day, thinking this, she looked down.
There at her feet was a wing.
She took it apart,
Cleaned the bones
And fitted it back together
Like a jigsaw.
She forgot about the soldier and his iron things.
She held up the wing to the sun
To see the cleverness in it.
And she said to herself
One day I'd like to build a metal bird machine
That flies in the sky
And gives people lifts in it.

   Lights down.
     Little Cog exits.

HUSH

Characters

Louise
Denise
Rosa
Tony
Colin
Dogboy

Hush was premièred at the Royal Court Theatre, London, on 6 August 1992, with the following cast:

Louise Marion Bailey
Denise Debra Gillett
Rosa Dervla Kirwan
Tony Stephen Dillane
Colin Will Knightly
Dogboy Andy Serkis

Directed by Max Stafford-Clark
Designed by Sally Jacobs
Lighting by Johanna Town
Sound by Bryan Bowen

Part One

The stage area is roughly divided into two parts. The beach and the house. The house is one room with a sofa, some cardboard boxes and a small, old, round sidetable which sits near the sofa. Both pieces of furniture are covered in a dust sheet. The room looks dusty, unlived in. The beach may encroach upon the house surrealistically.

SCENE ONE

The house, Louise enters. She stands for a moment in the room. She pulls off the dust sheet. She bundles it up. She exits.

SCENE TWO

The beach. Rosa and Denise sit on the beach. They look out to sea.

Denise I like beaches in winter.

Rosa More than in summer?

Denise Not more. But I like them.

Rosa I hate beaches.

   Pause.

Denise (*leans back*) That's better. (*Pause.*) Much better.

Rosa Better than what?

Denise Better than cleaning.

Rosa But you're a cleaner.

Denise I'm not a cleaner.

Rosa You clean things. That's what you do.

Denise That may be what I do at present. I may do that at present but that's not what I am.

Rosa What are you then? (*Pause.*) You're having a crisis.

Denise I am not.

Rosa You're stuck. Horribly stuck. Festering. Your youth is dwindling away.

Denise It is not.

Rosa Drip by drip.

Denise That's all you know. (*Pause.*) That's all you know because I'm leaving.

Pause.

Rosa Leaving?

Denise I've just got this weekend then I'm finished. I only decided on Tuesday. I've been meaning to tell you. (*Pause.*) I've got to do something. With my life. Start a new life.

Rosa Doing what?

Denise I'll think of something.

Rosa What?

Pause.

Denise I went to this woman last week. She's got this booth in Camden Market. She tells you things. She held my hand and she said 'do you mind if I swear?' She said

76

she swore when she got going. She said I should watch my back. I thought to myself 'is that symbolic?' But then I thought 'no, not for two pounds fifty'. (*Pause.*) She meant my lower back. She said me or my husband would have problems in that area.

Rosa You haven't got a husband.

Denise I know.

Rosa She sounds like a bucket of shit.

Denise I could have a husband. I could have. In the future.

  Pause.

Rosa Did she talk to any dead people?

Denise Not that I noticed.

Rosa They usually do. That sort. (*Pause.*) Bury me.

Denise What?

Rosa In the sand.

Denise What for?

Rosa Fun.

Denise That sand's grubby.

Rosa Go on.

Denise Unsalubrious.

Rosa If you don't do it I'm going to swallow a stone.

Denise You wouldn't?

Rosa I would. Then your new life would be unnecessarily complicated.

Denise That's blackmail.

Rosa Start with the feet.

Pause. Denise begins to bury Rosa.

Denise I don't know.

Rosa What?

Denise You. You're disturbed.

Rosa Did she swear then? That woman?

Denise No.

Rosa Didn't she even let a fuck slip?

Denise I don't think I inspired her.

Rosa What a disappointment, after all the build up.

Denise She said there was a stranger on my horizon. A ginger man.

Rosa How repulsive.

Denise What's wrong with that?

Rosa Pubes. Ginger pubes.

Denise Rosa!

Rosa Will you do my head?

Denise Your head?

Rosa Bury my head.

Denise What for?

Rosa The experience.

Denise It's a bit extreme.

Rosa Go on.

Denise You won't be able to breathe.

Rosa We can use that straw. (*She points to a straw in the sand.*)

Denise We don't know where it's been.

Rosa Don't be finicky.

Denise It's probably swarming with germs.

Rosa Give it here.

Denise I don't know how you can. (*She begins to bury Rosa's head.*) Don't let on to Louise.

Rosa Thus they committed her to the sand. And the deserts of time blew over her wiping out for ever from the eyes of men all last trace of her ethereal beauty.

Denise Put the straw in.

She covers Rosa up. She sighs. Lies down next to the mound. Pause.
Louise enters. She carries a young tree. She places it down.

Louise I bought a tree.

Denise sits up.

Denise Louise.

Louise Well?

Denise It's nice.

Louise It was bloody expensive. For a tree. I said to the man at the garden centre, 'Is this really the price?' and he said, 'yes', like he thought I was mad. I said I could go and dig up a tree for free.

Denise What did he say?

Louise He said that would be against the law.

Denise He was probably right. It probably is against the law.

Louise I know he was right. It's just the principle of the thing. A tree should be free or very cheap. (*Pause.*) Denise?

Denise Yes?

Louise I just wanted a word. (*Pause.*) You know you're always welcome to come down here at weekends. With us. Now we're getting the place sorted.

Denise Thanks.

Louise Also, also . . . you've been smashing.

Denise Oh . . . no. I haven't.

Louise I'm not just talking about dusting. I mean with Rosa. Us. It's been smashing. So any time you want a weekend by the sea . . .

Denise Thanks.

Louise Just let me know.

Denise Thanks.

Pause.

Louise (*noticing the mound*) What's that?

Pause.

Denise It's a mound.

Louise What's that sticking out of it?

Denise It's a straw.

Louise Am I missing something?

Denise It's Rosa. (*Pause.*) She wanted me to bury her.

Pause.

Louise Don't you think that's rather sick. In the circumstances?

Denise I didn't think.

Louise Obviously. Can she breathe?

Denise The straw.

Louise I see. It's incredibly unhygienic. She could get hepatitis.

Denise Sorry.

Louise approaches the mound.

Louise Rosa? (*Pause.*) I think you should come out now. (*Nothing happens. She removes the straw and throws it away. To Denise*) You better dig her up. (*She picks up the tree.*) I'm going to plant this somewhere it can be seen. From the sea. (*She exits.*)

Denise Shit.

Rosa breaks out of the sand.

Rosa I could have hepatitis.

Denise It's not funny.

Rosa If I did you'd feel guilty. You'd feel terrible. Your new life would be blighted.

Denise God knows what she thinks of me.

Rosa She thinks you're an idiot.

Denise It's like I've delivered a blow to my own karma.

Rosa You should have told her it was yoga. An advanced form of yoga.

Rosa gets up. She begins to dust herself down. Denise helps her.

I had sex.

Denise takes little notice of this. Continues to brush off sand.

Last time I was down here. Don't you want to know what it was like? His dick?

Denise Not particularly.

Rosa That's a lie. Everyone wants to know that sort of thing. I'll draw it for you in the sand if you like.

Denise Would he be likely to walk by and see it?

Rosa He wouldn't know it was his if he did. It's like not recognizing your own voice on tape.

Denise has finished brushing Rosa down. She sits down dispirited. Rosa draws in the sand.

Denise That's not to scale is it?

Rosa It's enlarged to the power of seventeen.

Denise I'm glad to hear it.

Rosa stands back to look at what she's drawn.

Rosa You don't believe me. You can't take anything in.

Denise You're not leaving that there. (*She rubs it out with her foot.*)

Rosa You'll miss me when you go. You'll miss my little ways.

SCENE THREE

The house. Louise and Tony. Louise is holding a spade. In the other hand she holds some sheets of A4 from which she is reading. Tony listens intently.

Louise . . . bulging red, pulsing red, engorged and red. Red red red. The eye of the traffic light blinked at him with meretricious self assurance. It seemed to signal to

him some preposterous urban omen, some secret sense of
his own deficiency; a ghastly plot to deprive him of his
'droit de seigneur'. He felt the raw sewage of panic
bubbling irresistibly and the next bit's scribbled out.

Tony Yes.

Louise Is that it?

Tony That's as far as I got.

Pause.

Louise Well . . . I think it's gripping.

Tony Gripping?

Louise Yes. Quite . . . gripping.

Tony Do you get the nightmare quality? Does the
nightmare quality come through?

Louise It certainly does come through. (*Pause.*) He's at the
traffic lights is he?

Tony It's just this chapter. I know at bone level if I can
crack it I'm home and dry. He's at his worst point you see.

Louise I see.

Tony He's struggling. Struggling. I'm making it bloody
difficult for him.

Louise (*twizzling the spade*) Good.

Tony But he survives. He survives. And on the way he
learns something about human goodness.

Louise (*looks closely at the spade*) Jolly good.

Tony The last page is almost filmic. He watches the sun
come up over the city. (*Pause.*) It's rather wonderful isn't it?
To think of all those people down the ages who have watched a sunrise with hope, with a sense of new possibilities.

Louise (*holding up the spade*) Do you think this is sufficient.

Tony Sufficient?

Louise For digging?

Tony I should think so.

Louise I bought a birch.

Tony A birch.

Louise I can remember Jo saying she liked them once. I don't know. She changed with the wind.

Pause.

Tony A birch is great. (*Pause.*) To me books are terribly important. They're like little mouths on the world. People need those, Louise.

Louise Yes.

Tony They need those like they need lungs.

Louise Yes.

Tony You're not just saying yes, are you? You do see what I mean?

Louise I have to go and dig a large hole shortly, Tony. I expect that's distracting me.

Tony Sorry.

Louise I can't tell you how much I've been longing for today. Longing to put it all behind me. A year. I've never known a year like it.

Tony Poor Louise.

Louise I want this whole business finished. Over.

Tony It is over. It's practically over.

84

Louise There's thirteen hours to go yet. I counted.

Tony That'll fly by. Fly. (*Pause.*) Louise? (*Pause.*) Do you still have faith in me? Faith that I can do it?

Louise I don't know how many times I can say it, Tony.

Tony Of course. Of course. (*Pause.*) I shouldn't ask. Not today.

Louise That's OK.

Tony Do you need any help? With the hole?

Louise I'd rather do it by myself. Catharsis.

Tony It's like with this character I'm writing. There's a struggle but he wins through. And in the end, things turn out his way. In the end things are OK. Things are, in the end.

Pause.

Louise Is anniversary the right word?

Tony There isn't another one.

Louise Doesn't seem right.

Tony That's the English language for you. Never a synonym when you need one.

Louise I'll be outside. (*She exits.*)

Tony picks up sheets of A4, scans them. Scribbles something in one of the margins. Thinks.
    Denise enters. She is carrying a bucket of water and a sponge. She sees Tony. Stops.

Denise Sorry. Are you working? I didn't realize.

Tony Don't mind me.

Denise I wouldn't like to think I was putting you off or anything. You know, interrupting the creative flow.

Tony You go ahead.

Denise takes the cloth off the small table.

Denise Dusty. (*Whispers.*) Sorry. (*She begins to wash the table with the cloth. She hums.*) I hummed. It was automatic. Shall I do this later?

Tony No. No. I'm just thinking really.

Denise I don't know how you think of things. I mean, how do you think of things?

Tony The million dollar question.

Denise I suppose it is. (*Pause.*) I wish I was good at something. (*She continues to wash over the table.*) Tennis or nursing. Something.

Tony You are. You are good at something.

Denise What?

Tony Everyone's good at something. (*Pause.*) For example, I know you as a cleaner. You're a very good cleaner.

Denise Oh God.

Tony Don't put yourself down, Denise. Where would we be without cleaners?

Denise I meant something like a vet or a solicitor. Something I could have enthusiasm for. I keep waiting. Waiting for something to come along. Only nothing comes along.

Tony It will. It will.

Denise It will?

Tony Things happen to people. They happen. People have a destiny. One morning you'll wake up and something will happen. You'll stumble on something inside you.

Denise Do you think?

Tony Absolutely. Absolutely. People have amazing resources inside of them. Amazing. I used to work with this old Polish guy. He told me that he'd bricked a woman up inside a chimney. Bricked her up for years inside a chimney.

Denise Why did he do that?

Tony She was a Jew and he saved her life. He hid her from the Nazis. He kept one brick loose and he used to pass food back and forth by means of removing the brick.

Denise He removed the brick?

Tony Yes. And amazingly, she survived.

Denise God.

Tony Yes.

Pause.

Denise What happened to her family?

Tony Well, they died. They died. But the point is she survived. That's because people have a lot of good in them. A lot of good which they find at the right moment.

Denise Yes, yes I see.

Tony The African elephant.

Denise Pardon.

Tony The African elephant will be saved in the nick of time by international co-ordination and agreement.

Denise Oh good.

Tony It's the same thing. Pulling that extra bit out of the bag and surprising even yourself.

Pause.

Denise I'm thinking of going to Tibet.

Tony Really?

Denise Yes.

Tony Fantastic.

Denise Yes. (*Pause.*) It's very spiritual. There's a lot of monks in Tibet.

Tony Ah.

Denise You can't turn around for the monks.

Tony So that's what you'll do?

Denise Do?

Tony When you leave us.

Denise Oh well. Yes. Maybe. I've got the brochures.

Tony Well. Good luck.

Denise Thanks.

Tony I think you're very brave. Setting out. It will be a whole new life.

Denise begins to cry.

Denise?

Denise Sorry. This is stupid. It's just now it's come to it. Going. It doesn't feel like I imagined it would.

Tony God. Look. I haven't got a handkerchief.

Denise That afternoon. That time . . . when we . . .

Tony Look . . .

Denise I shouldn't have brought it up.

Tony You're a lovely girl, Denise.

Pause.

Denise Sometimes I think 'Christ, what is going to happen to me?' I mean I haven't got anyone.

Tony You'll meet someone. You'll meet someone.

Pause.

Denise I'm sorry. I shouldn't have brought it up. About before.

Tony Don't worry. Don't worry. That's fine.

Denise begins cleaning the table once more.

Denise Apparently it's like a bowl.

Tony What is?

Denise Tibet. (*Pause.*) Apparently over the centuries all this good karma has collected in that bowl. Like rain. (*Pause.*) I'd like to sit right in the middle of that bowl like sitting at the bottom of a pool and feel all that good stuff wash over me. Till I was as clean as a stone in the sea. (*Pause.*) This table's coming up nice.

SCENE FOUR

At the edge of the beach Louise is digging. Rosa watches. The tree is beside them, ready to be planted.

Louise What do you think? (*Pause.*) The place. It's a nice spot.

Rose It's all right. (*Pause.*) She didn't like trees.

Louise I thought everybody liked trees.

Rosa I never heard her say she did. I never heard her say, 'I love trees.'

Louise It's not the sort of thing people do say. Not out

89

loud. Anyway I said like, like trees. You love people or dogs. You admire vegetation.

Rosa She never liked people.

Louise That's not true. You know that's not true.

Rosa She never liked you.

Louise We were sisters. Sisters fall out all the time.

Rosa Normal people like their sisters.

Louise Well, often people aren't normal. That's the tragedy of it.

Rosa You think she wasn't normal.

Louise I never said that. (*Pause.*) Rosa? (*Pause.*) We rub along all right together, don't we?

Pause.

Rosa Yes.

Louise Good. I'm glad.

Pause.

Rosa I hope that tree dies.

Louise You shouldn't say that. That's an awful thing to say. (*Pause.*) She didn't do it on purpose. (*Pause.*) The worst bit's over now. We can put the worst behind us. (*Pause.*) Do you want to help me plant it?

Rosa She fucked left right and centre. That house was a shit-hole when we lived there.

Louise It's rather heavy. I'll need someone to hold it. While I put the earth back.

Rosa You ought to get Tony or someone to give you a hand.

Rosa moves away. Sits facing away from Louise and the tree.

  Louise struggles with the tree alone.

Louise (*to herself*) Bastard tree. (*Louise manages to right the tree and stamps earth round it. She stands back.*)

Rosa Tony's here. Right in the nick of time.

  Tony and Denise enter.

Tony It's a smashing tree. (*Pause.*) You got it up on your own then?

  Pause.

Louise We should have thought of something. Something to say.

Tony We could have a few quotes. Poetry. (*Pause.*) I can't remember any.

  Pause.

Denise We could sing something.

Tony The Internationale.

Louise This isn't the time for flip remarks, Tony.

Tony Sorry.

Rosa I'm not singing anything.

Denise I meant like a hymn.

Louise Jo wasn't that way inclined.

Tony Man is descended from a sea-squirt. She sent Louise the article.

Denise Oh.

Tony Didn't she? Louise was in the Christian Union at college. Jo had a campaign.

Denise What's a sea-squirt?

Louise A sort of stomach on a stick that sucks up excreta from the sea bed.

Tony Jo knew how to mass her ideological troops. She could be very persuasive.

Louise I was an easy target.

Tony It put poor old Lu off.

Denise We're not really descended from sea-squirts?

Rosa Tony might be.

Louise I think we should get on with this. (*Pause.*) I think we should say anything we want. (*Pause.*) Hello. Anything. We'll do that.

Silence descends. They gather round the tree.

Tony. You go first.

Tony Do you think it should be me?

Louise Yes. Go on.

Tony takes a step or two forward towards the tree. Slight hesitation. Everyone watches.

Tony Hello Jo. It's me. Tony speaking. (*Pause.*) I'm still here. Still with Louise as you can probably guess. Louise has planted a pretty smashing tree here. For you actually, naturally. The house is getting a good clean up. I must say it's great being by the sea. I've always like the sea. (*Pause.*) This is a bit like an international call, isn't it? (*He laughs.*) I'm still slogging away at the old typewriter, every spare moment. Still teaching in between the real work, writing. Don't laugh but my last book *Salamander Days* got a mention in the *Sunday Times*. I don't think that was 'the book'. You know, not 'the book'. But who knows, maybe this next one? (*Pause.*) So . . . so . . . I can't think of much else. The world's still going round. 30km a second. (*Short laugh.*) Yes. We're all still trying. I realize . . . I shouldn't have said that earlier. About the sea . . . Sorry. Anyway, nice to chat. Over and out, Tony. (*He steps back.*) Was I all right?

Louise steps forward.

Louise Hello Jo. It's a year on. A year on. We all miss you. Rosa's here. She's with me now. (*Pause. She steps back.*) Rose?

Rosa does not move. Pause.
Denise steps forward.

Denise Jo. You don't know me. I've seen your photo. I help Louise out. Well, I'm just finishing. I did a bit of housecraft, you know, hoovering. I know Rosa. (*Pause.*) You've got a lovely daughter. (*Pause.*) I don't believe in God, but I do, you know, believe in something. Something more than just us. Just us here. I mean a force. A benevolent force. A force field even. Something big. Creative. Something that's in nature. I think whales are closer to it than we are. Closer to living it. I mean they don't do any damage, do they? They just do a lot of swimming and that's not because they're stupid. That's just the way they've evolved. They keep the same partner for ever. There's got to be something. I heard about this woman who kept seeing a cat out of the corner of her eye and there was nothing there. Nothing. Not a real cat. But something. You know. Something. (*She loses her thread. Steps back.*)

Louise Rosa?

Rosa I'm not talking to a tree.

Louise Why not?

Rosa It was in a shop a few hours ago.

Louise It might be a good thing. It might make you feel better.

Rosa When you die you rot. That's what she said. Slowly at first but then surprisingly quickly.

Louise Maybe we could leave you here alone. For a bit.

Rosa Do what you like.

Louise touches Rosa's arm. Rosa moves away. They leave Rosa by the tree. Rosa stares at the tree.

There was a little girl and she had a little curl right in the middle of her forehead. And when she was good she was very very good. And when she was bad she was horrid. (*Rosa kicks some sand at the tree. She exits.*)

SCENE FIVE

Denise alone on the beach. She makes a circle of stones in the sand. From her bag she takes a book. She takes off her shoes and places them with her bag outside the circle. She sits in the centre of the circle with the book. She thinks for a moment then closes her eyes and runs her hand over the pages of the book until she has chosen a place to open it. She hesitates once or twice then finally opens it. She opens her eyes, looks at the book. Turns it the right way round and reads.

Denise A tree is not a suitable place for a wild goose. (*She thinks.*) A goose? (*She closes her eyes. Repeats the process.*)

Colin enters.

(*opening her eyes, reads*) The tusk of a gelded boar brings good fortune.

Colin But is not easy to come by nowadays.

94

Denise starts.

Denise God! (*Pause.*) I was just . . . talking to myself.

Colin Can I see your book?

Denise My book?

Colin Yes.

Denise What for?

Colin Just to have a look.

Denise I don't know you.

Colin Is it new age?

Denise I don't know you from Adam.

Colin I'm just interested. (*He goes to step into the circle.*)

Denise Don't.

Colin What?

Denise Come in here. The circle.

Colin Oh. The circle. (*Pause.*) What happens if I do? Go in. (*Pause.*) Will I sprout horns?

Denise This is typical. A woman. A woman alone on a beach. It's like a red rag to a bull. To a man. (*Pause. She stands up and walks over to him, still keeping inside the circle.*) Remove yourself. Shrivel. Become extinct. (*Pause.*) Sometimes I look in men's eyes and know something's wrong. They've got eyes likes pebbles. (*Pause.*) Pissing dirty pebbles.

Pause.

Colin I was a friend of Jo's.

Pause.

Denise A friend of Jo's?

Colin Yes.

Denise Jo's?

Colin Yes.

Pause.

Denise Oh.

Colin Colin. (*Pause.*) I saw you earlier. With Rosa.

Pause.

Denise Do you live round here then?

Colin Not far.

Denise It's nice round here, isn't it?

Colin It's all right.

Denise The colours of the houses . . . are nice.

Colin I can't say I've given it much thought.

Denise That's understandable. As a visitor I'd notice that sort of thing you see. As a visitor. Whereas you, being an inhabitant would be more likely to take it for granted. As an inhabitant. (*Pause.*) The people are nice though. Friendly.

Colin A lot of rich bastards live round here. They creep down from the cities. To escape the mess they've made. It's like an infection.

Pause.

Denise That's an interesting way to look at it. An infection.

Pause.

Colin So you're a friend of Rosa's.

Denise Yes. In a way.

Colin That's nice for her.

Denise Nice?

Colin For her to have a friend.

Denise Oh. Oh. Yes. (*Pause.*) It's a lovely beach.

Colin It's filthy.

Denise Is it?

Colin And the sea. That's full of crap. Pollution.

Denise How awful. I mean. The sea.

Colin I don't know. There's a sort of justice in it. An equality in destruction. No one can enjoy it now. Not even the bourgeoisie.

Denise I suppose so. God, that's true. Yes. I can see that. The bourgeoisie. God. (*Pause.*) Here. (*She hands him her book.*) Open it. Any page you like.

He does so.

Read it.

Colin (*reading*) Published by Mushroom Press Limited, Northampton.

Denise Not that page. (*Pause.*) You ought to call round some time. See the house. For old times' sake.

Colin I'd like to. I may do that.

Denise I'm leaving tomorrow.

Colin Mind the circle.

Denise looks down. She has dislodged some of the stones.

Denise Oh that.

SCENE SIX

Somewhere along the beach.
Dogboy. He has a dog with him. This is theatrically imagined. He is playing with his dog. The dog leaps to fetch something he holds. Dogboy pulls his hand away each time.
Rosa approaches. Watches.

Rosa Is that your dog?

Dogboy continues playing with dog.

What's its name?

Pause. Dogboy still plays.

Dogboy Yelp.

Rosa That's the noise a dog makes.

Dogboy That was the idea.

Rosa It's an ugly dog.

Dogboy It doesn't have a very good diet.

Rosa You should feed it better.

Dogboy stops his game.

Dogboy What's it to you?

Rosa I could work for the RSPCA.

Dogboy Fuck the RSPCA. Spying eejits.

Rosa You're paranoid.

Dogboy And you're a polaroid.

Rosa Is that supposed to rhyme?

Dogboy Please yourself.

Pause.

Rosa You live on this beach. (*Pause.*) How d'you get a bath?

Dogboy A bath. Madam muck.

Rosa Madam muck yourself. (*Pause.*) My mother drowned in that sea.

Dogboy Was she a good swimmer?

Rosa Quite good.

Dogboy My dog's a fucking brilliant swimmer.

Rosa It might do it good to go in salt water.

Dogboy Maybe.

Pause.

Rosa I want to do it again.

Dogboy All right.

He lies down. Rosa undoes his flies, sits on him. She begins to move on top of him. After a bit she stops.

Rosa You're crying.

Dogboy So. I'm human.

Rosa That dog's whining.

Dogboy Sometimes I want to kick it when it does that.

Rosa You wouldn't though.

Dogboy No. I'd feel bad afterwards.

Rosa climbs off him.

Rosa I might as well go then.

Dogboy I'm looking for a cave.

Rosa What cave?

Dogboy A dry, sandy cave.

Rosa There's no caves round here.

Dogboy There could be.

Rosa I used to live down here. I lived down here years. I never saw a cave.

Dogboy You can't see the best caves from the outside. (*Pause.*) I tell you what. This dog is a bloody good watchdog. Aren't you girl? Eh? When I sleep, she watches. Don't you girl? Eh?

Rosa There's no caves.

Dogboy begins to sharpen a stone against another stone.

Dogboy This is how people made tools. How they made tools in the old days. Stone on stone. Stone on stone. They made things with blades. That's how they slit throats. Animal throats. They did it at the neck where the skin's soft. Where the blood is. Where there's a lot of blood to come out. Blood and air would bubble out. (*He continues to sharpen the stone.*) I've been working on this. Look. (*He shows Rosa.*) You can touch it. Touch the edge.

She doesn't touch it.

Go on.

She touches it.

Ow! Sharp, eh? Hurts. (*He lays it flat against his cheek.*) Warm. It's warm. (*He begins to sharpen it again.*)

Rosa We should have used something. (*Pause.*) Precautions. Before. When we did it.

Dogboy How old are you?

Rosa Fifteen and one month.

Dogboy You're under age.

Rosa Only legally.

Dogboy The law's the law.

Pause.

Rosa What would you do if I was? If I swelled up bigger and bigger?

Dogboy I'd see you all right.

Rosa How would you?

Dogboy You'll see what I'll do.

Rosa I'd have to leave school.

Dogboy You'd go back though. After. There's no prospects without an education.

Pause.

Rosa You couldn't do anything. If I was.

Dogboy You'll see. What I'll do.

Rosa You've only got a stone. A stone and a dog.

Dogboy I've got something else.

Rosa What?

Out of his coat he brings a magazine.

Let's have a look.

She reaches for it. He whisks it away.

Dogboy In a bit.

Rosa Is it filthy?

Dogboy It's mine. There's people in here, their faces shine.

Rosa That's the paper. The quality of the paper.

Dogboy Shine. Like saints.

Rosa It's the paper. Give it to me.

Dogboy Wait.

She grabs it.

Rosa (*looking at the magazine*) Do you read it?

Dogboy Yes.

Rosa Fucking queer.

Dogboy Get lost.

Rosa You stole it.

Dogboy I found it.

Rosa Put your hands in dirty rubbish.

Dogboy I found it.

She hits him with the magazine.

Rosa Queer bastard.

Dogboy Don't hit me.

She hits him with it again.

I'll set the dog on you.

Rosa Shiny faces. (*She hits him again.*)

Dogboy Get off!

Rosa Fucking queer. Fucking queer in the head. (*She hits him.*)

Dogboy Don't hit me.

Rosa You'll be crying soon. (*She begins to tear up the magazine.*)

Dogboy It's mine.

Rosa Boo hoo. (*She continues to tear it.*)

Dogboy Don't tear it!

Rosa Fucking queer bastard.

Dogboy Fuck you.

Rosa throws the magazine to the ground.

Rosa Crying bastard. Like saints. Don't you know anything? You couldn't do anything if I was. Could you?

Dogboy kneels down. Smoothes out a bit of the magazine. Begins to read.

Dogboy Have the days of sticky-back plastic passed us by? Covering old jars with this new range of designer plastics performs a miracle of recycling and can create a matching set of storage containers for the cheap and cheerful kitchen. (*Pause.*) Sometimes I see people. In their windows. Sometimes they're black bastards. Sometimes they're women or men in shirts. They close their curtains and they yawn. Sometimes I close my eyes and I see myself going in. Often they're asleep. I've got my stone in my hand or in my pocket. I stick it into their hearts or their necks. (*He goes over to Rosa. He touches her stomach.*) Is it in there?

SCENE SEVEN

The house.
Louise is sorting out stuff in the boxes. While she does this Tony is typing on a small manual typewriter. He sits at the small table Denise has cleaned earlier. He draws a page out of his typewriter. He looks at it. Laughs.

Louise Is that a funny bit?

Tony This guy. I've got this guy in his bedroom. I've

decided to keep the place vague. Eastern European.

Louise It's not vague if you happen to come from Eastern Europe.

Tony Queues, greyness, a tendency to weep. You know.

Louise Sounds like London.

Tony Anyway, this guy has just been overcome with paint fumes. He's stumbling about and he mistakenly gets into his wardrobe which has a faulty catch . . . and he can't get out. (*Laughs. Pause.*) You have to read it really.

Louise is unfolding a banner which she has taken out of one of the boxes. She reads:

Louise 'Women unite to reclaim the night.' This would probably fetch something on the memorabilia market. Jo never threw anything out. She was either a hoarder or extremely disorganized.

Tony The paint fumes are an analogy. The bewilderment of new ideas. What will happen when the man comes out of the wardrobe?

Louise (*folding banner*) He steps in a paint tin?

Tony This is an amazing time, Louise. An amazing time to be living in. Huge empires are breaking up. It's like the end of the ice age. Watching the ice cracking. All warm-blooded species rejoice!

Louise holds up a jumper with a huge CND symbol on it.

Louise Do you think Jo ever wore this? (*She examines it.*) It's a monstrosity. I expect she did.

Tony Recently people have died for their ideas. Laid down in front of tanks and the tanks have rolled over them and they've been squashed.

Louise I don't expect they imagined that would happen. Not when they lay down.

Tony But they took the risk. That's the human spirit. It gives me a great sense of optimism.

Louise has tried on the jumper. It is very big. It reaches her knees.

Louise Subtle, isn't it? (*Pause.*) All this is going, Tony. Everything. Today. I can't stand this stuff hanging around any more. We've come down here the odd weekend and it's like we've been afraid to touch anything. We've been tip-toeing around, thinking things are sacred. This isn't a shrine. It's my house now, mine and Rosa's. This is day one, Tony. Everything has to be dead and buried from today. That's what I want.

Tony What I want is for this book to be better than the last. That's what I want. (*Pause.*) Then it will reach more people.

Louise Everything's so dusty. Dust is mostly human skin. Flakes of human skin. Did you know that? (*Pause.*) She's been with me a year now, Rosa. A year. But it's not right. There's something between us. Distance. Why should there be? Sometimes I look at the back of her head and my throat aches. (*Pause.*) She knows I'm lying.

Tony You're not lying.

Louise I cast a light on things. A comfortable light. That's a deception. You can smell that. Rosa can.

Tony You took the best option. And in all probability you were right.

Louise You can't build something on a lie. Its roots keep humping up the earth.

Tony Jo went swimming. That's all we know.

Louise That's not all we know. (*Pause.*) She had

problems. We know she had problems. Living down here.
She hid down here. Dreaming. Living off ideas. How do
you explain seventeen empty cans of baked beans in the
washing machine? She went up and down like a yo-yo.
There's a name for that.

Tony She was obviously a very untidy woman. That
doesn't prove anything. It's supposition.

Louise What about the phone call? Days before she
phoned me. She said she hadn't bothered to get dressed for
three days. Three days. She said that. She said her hair was
going grey. She was depressed about the Gulf. God knows.
Something. Those aren't suppositions, Tony.

Tony Everyone was depressed about the Gulf. It was a
highly inflammable situation.

Louise Stop sitting on the fence, Tony.

Tony It's a question of accuracy, Louise. We just don't know
what happened. You couldn't say anything now anyway.

Louise Why not?

Tony Well. I think that would be a little insensitive. Not to
say irresponsible.

Louise Don't you understand? It's coming between us. Me
and Rosa. The lie is ruining everything. (*Pause.*) Your book.

Tony Yes?

Louise When you ask me my opinion, what do you
expect?

Tony I expect the truth.

Louise And what if I thought it was turgid, you know,
distended beyond its natural size by watery substances?

Pause.

106

Tony I don't see the point of all this.

Louise What would you expect then?

Tony I'd expect your honest opinion.

Louise You wouldn't rather I lied? A kind but cowardly act? Because that's the choice.

Tony I'd still want the truth.

Louise Naturally. Anyone would.

Pause.

Tony Are you trying to tell me something?

Louise Because that's the choice.

Tony What I've shown you. You hate it don't you?

Louise Do you really want to know?

Tony Yes.

Louise Really?

Pause.

Tony Yes.

Louise You see. People need truth, Tony. Otherwise they resent you. That's understandable.

Tony My book?

Louise I haven't got the guts. The guts to tell Rosa.

Pause.

Tony What about the book?

Louise I'm not talking about that now.

Tony You don't understand. I lie awake thinking about that book. Turning it over and over. It's my contribution,

Louise. To everything. That's why I do it. To contribute. If
I didn't do that who would I be?

Louise You'd be a teacher.

Tony I think I'll go out for a bit.

Louise I was making a point. That's all. A point.

He gets up, exits. Pause.
    Louise continues to sort out Jo's stuff. She pulls out a
dressing gown, past its best, a pink, silky 1930s affair.
She examines it.

This was falling apart. It's rotten under the arms. I expect
you sat around in this, fundraising for a Nicaraguan
women's rug weaving collective. (*She smells it.*) It smells.
Smells of you. (*Pause.*) The trouble is your stuff's falling
apart. (*Pause.*) The trouble is you're not quite gone. You're
still in the dust. Floating about in the dust. (*Pause.*) This
place was a mess, Jo. You make a mess and then you leave
me to clear it up. (*Pause.*) It's not so much you, how you
lived, I was thinking of Rosa. (*Pause.*) That name. Calling
her that. It's quite a lot to live up to, Jo. Political martyr-
dom. I used to watch her when she was small. I used to
think I'd be quite happy for my child not to smear banana
on the living room carpet. Something ordinary, like that.
But that name's a weight, Jo, a weight. (*Pause.*) Did you
ever think that she might be more like me? Not like you.
Like me. (*She takes off the jumper and stuffs it with the*
dressing gown back into the box.) The trouble with you,
Jo, is that you're destructive. The things you touched.
Maybe it was just as well. Just as well, what happened.
There. I've said it now. I've said it. I didn't want to say it.

Pause. Rosa enters.

Rosa?

Rosa I need something. From the kitchen.

Louise Rosa. (*Pause.*) I just wanted to say . . . what I wanted to say was that sometimes . . . sometimes I haven't been as honest with you . . . as honest as perhaps I should have been. But I wanted you to know that from today . . . from today you can ask me anything and that from today I will be honest with you. Tell you. (*Pause.*) About Jo. Anything. (*Pause.*) Earlier by the tree, we were talking. Remember?

Pause.

Rosa There is something.

Louise Yes?

Rosa Would you ever have a baby?

Pause.

Louise What brought that up?

Rosa Would you?

Pause.

Louise I can't. I can't have one.

Rosa Why?

Pause.

Louise I did something. Something stupid once. (*Pause.*) I was young. I didn't understand things. Well, I understood them but I couldn't believe they were happening to me. I missed my time, twice, three times.

Rosa What did you do?

Louise This is twenty years ago. I was at college. I went to my room and hit myself. I hit myself here. (*She indicates.*) I hit myself over and over. After a bit I started to bleed. It was a very stupid thing to do. I did myself quite a bit of damage. I didn't go to my doctor soon enough. Unfortunately. (*Pause.*) So.

Denise enters.

Denise Hi.

Rosa The kitchen. I better go.

She exits.
Louise goes back to the boxes. Picks one up. Pause.

Denise I've been on the beach. Ages. Looking at the sea. It's incredible, isn't it? A human thing. That something can happen to you at a certain moment. At the right moment something lifts you. I met a man on the beach. I mean it's not as if I'm down here all the time or anything. I mean it is odd, isn't it? That just this morning I had a feeling . . . not a good feeling but then something can happen, happen just like that. Like fate. And I feel different. Full. It's as if something can come along.

Louise A man can come along.

Denise If you like. And then without me doing anything . . . It's weird. It's incredible isn't it?

Louise I wouldn't know. I don't have a religious faith.

Denise Not religious. Like fate. Brilliant.

Louise exits with box.

Brilliant.

SCENE EIGHT

Beach. Rosa finds Dogboy hunched on the sand. He is not wearing his coat. Pause.

Rosa Where's your dog?

Dogboy It's run off.

Rosa Has it?

Dogboy Or someone's done its head in with a rock. There's a lot of them about. Rocks.

Pause.

Rosa Where's your coat?

Dogboy Dunno. Up the beach.

Pause.

Rosa I bought you something. (*She hands him a sandwich. Pause.*) Say ta.

Dogboy takes a bite. Swallows.

Dogboy I feel cold.

Rosa You shouldn't leave your coat lying about.

Dogboy I feel cold all the time.

Rosa You shouldn't have left it.

Dogboy drops his sandwich in the sand.

Dogboy I've dropped it.

Rosa Didn't you want it?

Dogboy It was an accident. It'll have sand on it now. I don't like it when they get sand on them.

Rosa You never wanted it.

Dogboy I did. I'll eat it now. See. (*He begins to eat it where it lies. Animal like.*)

Rosa Not like that. Not like that. You're fucking mental. Brain dead mental.

Dogboy Your mother was mental. She drowned in that sea.

Pause. Rosa exits.

Come back. Come back. I don't mean anything. (*Pause.*)

Something's coming. Something's coming. I can smell it. It has wet teeth. Terrible. Think something. Think it. Think anything. Think it now. Think it. Keep it off me. Can't keep it off me. Can't stop it. Can't stop it. (*He gives a cry. He suddenly convulses as if something has possessed him.*)

SCENE NINE

The house. Evening.
　　The boxes are gone. There is a lamp on. Louise enters with a vase of flowers, which she puts on the small table. She exits.
　　Denise enters tentatively. She is over-dressed for the occasion. She is wearing a short dress. She is anxious about this. She perches on the edge of the sofa. She carries a handbag.
　　Louise enters with a bowl of peanuts, which she will place on the table. She sees Denise.

Louise Oh! That's a nice dress.

Denise It's too much, isn't it?

Louise Too much?

Denise You know. Just too much. Uncasual. Over the top. Tarty. Throwing it about.

Louise Well, I wouldn't say so. (*Pause.*) Are you expecting anyone?

Denise Oh no, no, no. (*Pause.*) No. (*Pause.*) It's just, if this man wants to call round some time, if he wants to, he might just call round tonight. It might be that tonight might be a good time seeing as I'm leaving tomorrow. Mightn't it?

Louise I see.

Denise God, I feel nervous. My hands are shaking.

Louise Is that the prospect of travelling?

Denise What? (*Pause. She opens her bag and brings out a bottle of wine.*) I got a bottle of wine. It's Bulgarian. Do you want some?

Louise No thanks.

Denise Oh go on. Otherwise I'll just drink it all myself and get slaughtered.

Louise Well. All right then. Just a glass.

Denise I'll get them. (*She gets glasses. Sits back down. While opening the bottle:*) Sometimes you remind me of a train.

Louise Thanks very much.

Denise I meant a train on its tracks. (*Pause.*) A train going, going, going. (*Pause.*) It's meant as a compliment. I used to see you leaving for work in the mornings when I had early starts. You had a briefcase and a raincoat and I'd think there goes a woman with enthusiasm. Then I'd imagine you coming back at night. You'd sit down and have a gin.

Louise There's quite a lot to be done, in between the setting off and the gin.

Denise Oh, I know. I know. (*Pause. She hands Louise a glass. Takes one for herself.*) Cheers. (*Pause.*) I meant to ask you. Do you think I'd be good. Any good in a job like yours?

Louise On a magazine?

Denise Yes.

Louise Have you got any qualifications?

Denise How d'you mean?

Louise Any qualifications?

Pause.

Denise Not really. (*Pause.*) Once I started on a jewellery design course. But it was ever so fiddly. After a bit I just went off it. I left one Friday night and never found the enthusiasm to return. I've matured a lot since then though.

Louise I thought you were set on going to Tibet.

Denise For when I got back I was thinking. (*Pause.*) That was the door.

Tony enters with his typewriter.

It's Tony.

Louise (*to Tony*) What's that?

Tony It's a typewriter

Louise I can see that.

Tony It's got rather cold upstairs. My fingers were going numb. (*He puts typewriter on small table.*)

Louise Aren't you being a little anti-social?

Tony I'm not disturbing anyone am I?

Louise I don't particularly want to sit here listening to you clatter away on that thing.

Tony I'll sit in the corner.

Louise I'll still be able to hear it from the corner.

Tony I'm at rather a significant juncture.

Louise I remain unmoved.

Pause.

Tony All right. Since there appear to be strong objections I'll proceed in pencil. You shouldn't be able to hear that unless you're listening very hard for it.

Louise You still won't be joining in.

Tony Joining in what?

Louise Conversation. The general free flowing exchange of ideas. You know, the thing people do in your books a lot. Sit opposite each other and talk.

Tony Fine. (*He sits down, folds his arms. Waits. Silence.*)

A long pause.

Denise Once I got really pissed. Really pissed at this party and then I got really hungry, really hungry, you know, like you do after drinking and so I devoured a bowl of peanuts. A whole bowl, to myself. (*Pause.*) And then I vomited the lot back up. I sort of regurgitated them. The thing is, the thing is, they came out whole. I must just have swallowed them down without any sort of chewing. Later someone remarked that they shot out like bullets. Ping ping. Ping. (*Pause.*) I was a bit depressed at the time.

Tony I'm afraid I don't have any vomit stories.

Louise You're just not trying.

Pause.

Denise Was that the door?

Tony Are we expecting someone?

Denise and Louise No.

Denise jumps up.
Rosa enters.
Denise sits back down.

Denise Rosa.

Rosa There's boxes outside. Boxes of Jo's stuff.

Louise I've been clearing things out. Nothing precious. Nothing we would have wanted to keep.

Rosa I don't want to keep anything. I just saw the boxes.

Louise It looks better in here, doesn't it?

Denise It must be nearly half past. Nearly half past by now.

Rosa Is someone coming?

Tony/Louise/Denise No.

Pause.

Rosa We should burn them.

Louise Burn them?

Rosa The boxes. Pile them up and burn them.

Louise I was thinking of sending them to Oxfam.

Rosa It's quicker to burn them.

Louise It would be quick.

Tony You're not going to burn them?

Louise It's not illegal, Tony.

Tony Rosa doesn't really want to. Do you, Rosa?

Rosa Yes, I do. (*to Louise*) Let's do it now.

Louise Now?

Rosa Then we won't have to see them again. Think of them.

Louise Like a big finish?

Rosa A big fire.

Louise picks up a box of matches. She shakes them.

Louise Matches!

Tony It's a bit of a Nazi impulse, isn't it, Louise? They burnt books.

Louise Don't tempt me.

They exit.

Tony Sometimes I wonder whether she has any respect for my work whatsoever?

Pause.

Denise The reason I'd been depressed was because I'd been working at this sandwich-making job. I was living with this bloke and we were making sandwiches in his flat. At first I really threw myself into it. I experimented with fillings, I bought a butter dish. We used to drive round delivering sandwiches to local businesses only quite often we never got any orders. We ate quite a lot of sandwiches on those occasions. That dealt quite a blow to my enthusiasm I can tell you. Not to mention the fact that I wasn't getting the correct balance of amino acids in my diet. And that can lead to personality disorders. Like shoplifting or slimming. Then one day we found a cockroach lying upside down in a giant size tub of margarine. It wasn't me that left the lid off. That was when the infestation started. You can never be alone with an infestation. Soon after that he left me. He walked out leaving rent arrears and twenty-seven kilos of cheddar. I lay in bed weeping for days. I don't know if what we had was love but it did provide light relief from all the buttering. That was before I became a Buddhist. I used to watch the cockroaches basking on the walls. They do say in the event of a nuclear holocaust cockroaches will survive to inherit the earth. They used to crawl around in a superior manner as if they knew they could survive intense heat and I couldn't. Cocky bastards. The thing is, I'd never go through that now. Be used like that. Because now I'm different. Transformed by experience. (*Pause.*) What time is it?

Tony Seven forty-five.

Denise It's not too late is it? I mean if you were going to drop in unexpectedly on someone it's not too late?

Tony I don't suppose so.

Denise Good. (*Pause.*) Sometimes I wonder what happens. What happens to people who can't find enthusiasm for things. The way things are. (*Pause.*) Of course there's always acupuncture.

Rosa and Louise enter.

Louise We've got a blaze going.

Rosa A fire.

Louise It's all going up.

Rosa Burning.

Louise It was fast. It went up fast.

Rosa All the sparks. Flying up.

Louise puts her arm round Rosa.

Louise It's a good end. A good end.

Denise The door. That was it. The door. I heard it. God. How do I look? (*She hurries out.*)

Denise returns. She is followed by Dogboy. He stands in the doorway. He is naked. He holds his stone. He is muddy, bloody.
Dogboy barks. Pause. He barks again.

He was there. At the door.

Tony Jesus.

Dogboy barks.

He's naked.

Louise Go away!

Dogboy barks.

Go away!

Dogboy does not move.

Part Two

SCENE TEN

The house. A little later.

Dogboy is sitting on the floor. He has a blanket over him. He seems vacant. Denise is watching him intently. She stands holding her shoe in one hand, as if to use the heel as a weapon. She is poised. Rosa stands well in the background as if to disassociate herself. She watches too. She gives no help to Denise. Dogboy makes a soft grunting noise. Denise jumps. She looks over to the door. No one comes. She resumes her watch. Dogboy gives a small whine.

Denise (*calling*) Louise! (*Pause. Nothing happens.*) Fuck.

    Pause.

Dogboy (*looking at her*) Smell. (*Pause.*) Smell. Got bigger and bigger. Took me over like an itch. Sea stinks fish. Air stinks salt. Sand stinks sun and dirt. Smell drags me. Leads me circles. Paths and paths. Found old belt. Smells dead horse. Smell pulls me like God.

Denise Shut up.

    Dogboy growls.

Louise! (*to Rosa*) Where is she?

    He growls again.

I'm warning you. (*Pause. She looks towards the door.*) I've hit people before. I'm not afraid to. I've drawn blood.

    Dogboy growls.

Quite a lot of blood.

Dogboy gets up and snatches the shoe from Denise with a bite. Holds it in his mouth. She gives a cry.

Louise!

Dogboy growls and shakes the shoe from side to side in his mouth.
  Louise and Tony enter.

He's got my shoe. He snatched it. He was growling.

Tony Did you provoke him in any way?

Louise Of course she didn't.

Denise I didn't. (*to Rosa*) Did I?

Tony He seemed perfectly calm when we left.

Louise Well he's not calm now. (*to Dogboy*) Give that back.

Dogboy backs away. Whines a little.

Give it back.

Tony Shouting at him won't get you anywhere. (*He approaches Dogboy.*) Drop it. Drop it.

Dogboy drops it.

There.

Louise Bravo.

Tony picks up the shoe and gives it to Denise, who takes it gingerly.

That was the easy bit. (*Pause.*) Rosa. I think you should go upstairs.

Rosa Why?

Louise Please don't argue. It's just for the best.

Rosa exits ungraciously.

Tony I'm not sure I can do this, Louise.

Louise Do I have to do it?

Tony It's not a question of who does it. It's a question of do we do it at all?

Louise It's either that or turn him out for the night and lock the doors. You choose.

Tony It's raining out. It's started to rain.

Louise Well then, I don't see why we just don't phone the police.

Tony They'll only throw him into a cell.

Louise Probably the best place for him.

Tony I couldn't have that on my conscience, Louise.

Louise Then there's no alternative.

Tony It just doesn't seem right.

Louise There's a fifteen-year-old girl in this house and she's in my care. I have a duty towards her. I've asked you to come up with another solution and I may say that you've failed dismally on that score. This is real life, Tony, not one of your novels and in real life things actually really happen and one actually really responds.

Tony The thing about my novels, Louise, is that they tend to convey a spirit of optimism. Trust and optimism. Both of which are sadly lacking here.

Louise Give me the ropes.

Pause.

Tony I'll do it. I'd just like it publicly noted that I do it with a great deal of reluctance. (*He approaches Dogboy.*)

Hello. (*Pause.*) Look. I've got some rope.

He pulls the rope out of his pocket and shows it to Dogboy. Dogboy pats the bit of hanging rope with his hand. It swings.

Rope. And I think I'd better explain that although this goes against quite a few of my deeply held principles I'm afraid I'm going to have to restrain you just for tonight.

Dogboy grabs hold of the rope.

Ah. He's got hold of the rope, Louise.

Louise Yes, I can see that.

Dogboy begins to pull on the rope.

Tony I think he wants a game.

Louise For goodness' sake.

Tony (*to Dogboy*) Actually, this is the rope I was meaning to employ.

Dogboy pulls the rope harder.

He's pulling the rope quite hard now.

Louise Well, pull it back.

Tony does so. A small tug of war ensues. Dogboy suddenly lets go. Tony loses his balance.

Now you've had the game. Perhaps you can get on with it.

Dogboy offers Tony his hands.

Tony He's offering his hands. I think he understands.

Louise Of course he understands.

Tony begins to tie Dogboy's hands in front of his body.

Not in front of his body, Tony. If you tie his hands in front of his body he'll be able to undo his feet.

Tony I don't think he'd do that.

Louise Unless you do it properly there's absolutely no point in doing it at all.

Dogboy puts his hands behind his back. Tony ties them. Tony begins on his feet.

Tony This whole thing's ridiculous.

Louise He growled at Denise just now. Didn't he, Denise?

Denise Yes, he did. Grrr, like that. Then he leapt at me.

Louise See.

Tony I can't believe that I'm spending my Saturday night tying a man up.

Louise It's no use making me out to be a monster. I don't like it any more than you do. I'm just not prepared to take any risks.

Tony Well, it's done now. It's done.

Louise Put the blanket over him, so he's warm.

Tony (*tucking the blanket round him*) There you go.

Louise Someone should sleep down here for tonight. Just in case.

Tony Just in case what?

Denise I will. I'll sleep down here. I don't mind. We could still get a visitor, late. I'll sleep on the sofa.

Louise Thanks. (*Pause.*) Everything was supposed to be over today. Now there's this. Something dragging on. It's like Jo doesn't want everything to be over. It's as if she's sent something. To vex me. (*She exits.*)

*Denise takes the bottle of wine and sits on the sofa. She
drinks some of the wine straight from the bottle.
Dogboy licks Tony's hand.*

Tony He's quite a playful chap, isn't he? (*He exits.*)

*Denise looks at Dogboy, drinks some more.
Pause.*

Denise You know what I was thinking. I was thinking if
you were driving a car, through say, slowly moving traffic
and you saw me, walking. What would you think? (*Pause.*)
Would you think 'that looks like an attractive person, a
person who it would be good to spend an evening with' or
would you think 'that looks like a boring person with a
funny haircut'? What do you think? Because that was
what I was thinking. (*Pause.*) I don't know why I'm asking
you. Look at you. You're a bloody state. How did you get
like that? You've let yourself go. There's no need for that.
(*Pause. She goes over and lifts up the blanket.*) It's not
much to write home about. Is it? When you come to look
at it. (*She puts down the blanket.*) Still. When you're in
love it changes all that doesn't it? The other person
becomes sort of godlike and you feel sort of godlike and it
lifts you into another world. (*Pause.*) Still, it's not much is
it, close up. (*She gets back on the sofa. Lies down.*) There's
got to be more than that. Something else I could feel
passionate about. A great painting or a political
movement. (*Pause.*) People only join political movements
so they can get off with someone. (*She closes her eyes.*)

SCENE ELEVEN

*The same. Early morning.
Denise lies on the sofa asleep. An empty bottle on the
floor beside her. The lights come up a bit. Rosa enters*

124

quietly, surveys the situation. She walks quietly over to Dogboy. She kneels next to him. Whispers.

Rosa See that light. That's morning coming up over the sea. Morning comes up that way. Orange. And the sea's dark, dark. (*Pause.*) You keep your mouth shut. I'm keeping my mouth shut. (*She pats her stomach.*) Just remember that. Bad dog. (*She exits softly.*)

SCENE TWELVE

The same morning.
   Lights fully up. We can see Denise more clearly. She looks wrecked. Pause.
   Colin enters.

Colin Hello? Hello?

Denise wakes. Orients herself. Colin comes fully into the room.

The door was open. (*Pause.*) It's not too early is it? To pop in?

Pause.

Denise I must look crap.

Colin I came to see the house, for old times' sake.

Denise For old times' sake?

Colin Yes.

Denise I'm leaving today. Starting my new life.

Colin Well. Good luck.

Denise Thanks. (*Pause.*) You spoke to me first.

Colin Pardon?

Denise On the beach. You spoke to me first. I didn't ask you to.

Colin No.

Denise No. (*Pause.*) You approached me. I was minding my own business. I was quite happy.

Pause.

Colin It's a while. Since I've been here. (*Pause.*) Quite a while.

Denise Last night. (*Pause.*) Last night I thought you might, well . . .

Colin Well?

Denise Pop in. I thought you might pop in.

Colin Well, I popped in this morning. Does it make any difference?

Denise No. Absolutely no fucking difference whatsoever. (*Pause.*) Anyway, I'm going to Tibet. (*Pause.*) Would you go to Tibet?

Colin Not personally.

Denise Yet you'd be quite happy for me to go!

Colin No one's forcing you are they?

Pause.

Denise What's in Tibet? Lots of long dry roads and a load of daft monks.

Colin Not to mention a military occupation.

Pause.

Denise A ginger man.

Colin What?

Denise Nothing.

Pause.

Colin Perhaps I'd better call in another time.

Denise Go on then. Go.

Colin Well. Good luck with everything.

Denise I thought. (*Pause.*) I thought the only thing, the only thing was two people, two people together. I thought the only thing was looking at someone and them looking at you. In your eyes. Close up. That thing. What else is there? Just to be held. Held. I haven't got enthusiasm for anything else. All my life people have been avoiding me or taking bits and leaving the rest. I've had to force people. Force them to be with me. That's not right. Why's that? I thought you looked at me. That's what I thought. I thought you watched me in that way.

Pause. Dogboy whines faintly.

Colin What's that noise? (*He notices Dogboy in the blanket.*) I didn't see him. Is he sleeping?

Rosa and Louise enter from outside.

Denise Oh fuck!

Pause.

Louise It's too late. I've planted it.

Colin What?

Louise The tree. I planted it yesterday. (*Pause.*) Is there something wrong with it? Is that why you're here? To deliver tidings of a leaf virus?

Colin I . . .

Louise Because it's not coming up again. It comes up

again over my dead body. You shouldn't sell dud trees.

Colin It's not a dud.

Rosa That's Colin.

Colin I knew Jo.

Louise Oh. So this is a social call. I was confused. Yesterday you sold me a tree.

Colin I had a hunch you might be Louise.

Louise (*to Denise*) We've been out. Looking at what's left of the fire.

Colin I've been wanting to talk.

Louise We're thinking of using the ashes for the garden. They're supposed to be good for gardens.

Colin It won't take long.

Louise It's a bit hectic this morning.

Denise (*to Colin*) You must think I'm stupid.

Colin (*to Louise*) I've been wanting to talk to Rosa.

Louise I'm sorry. We're busy.

Denise (*to Colin*) You must think 'God, she's stupid'. Mustn't you?

Colin (*to Denise*) No.

Denise God.

Louise (*to Colin*) Perhaps you should write a letter. Put it in the post.

Colin It needs to be said face to face.

Denise (*to Colin*) You never wanted me, did you? You wanted to talk to them.

Colin (*to Louise*) We met earlier.

Louise I gathered.

Denise You were lovers. You and Jo. Lovers. (*Pause.*)
Pebbles. Bloody pebbles. I was right. (*She exits.*)

Pause.

Colin Hello, Rosa.

Rosa He's a communist, Colin. He always wears those
trousers.

Colin We spent a lot of time together. Me, Jo and you.
Didn't we? Remember once we tried to build a boat?

Rosa We used to switch the lights out when he called
round. Then we'd lie on the floor, me and Jo. We were
laughing. We used to bite our arms so he wouldn't hear us.

Colin We fell out. We fell out near the end. Before that
we were close. We saw eye to eye on things. (*Pause.*)
Rosa. I want to talk to you. About Jo.

Louise She doesn't want to talk about that.

Colin Can't she answer for herself? (*Pause.*) Look. I
didn't come here to fight. It's just that I've been thinking.
About what Jo would have wanted.

Louise We've no idea what she would have wanted.

Colin What Jo would have wanted for Rosa.

Louise Rosa is happy where she is.

Colin I'm not saying she's not happy. I'm saying that Jo
lived in a certain way.

Louise I know how she lived. This house was a health
hazard.

Colin I'm not talking about housework. I'm talking

about principles. You have coffee in this house.

Louise Is that some sort of mistake?

Colin I don't suppose you've spared a thought to the plantation workers. The conditions they have to endure?

Louise I'm sure they're awful.

Colin That's right. There's a case of a woman who organized a union meeting and was dead one week later. She was found by her daughter tied to a tree. Both her breasts had been cut off.

Pause.

Louise What exactly are you trying to say?

Colin Jo wouldn't have coffee in the house. She was boycotting it.

Louise I'm sure that had a devastating effect on imports.

Colin Rosa knows what I'm talking about.

Louise Well, now you've said your bit, lectured us on the evils of the coffee bean, perhaps you could go.

Colin You see, Jo and I talked. We talked of this eventuality. If something happened to her.

Louise Something happened to her a year ago. It's too late to change anything now.

Colin I wanted to wait. Until Rosa could make a decision for herself.

Louise What decision?

Colin A decision about how she wanted to live. I want you to know you've got a choice, Rosa. That you've still got friends down here. People who thought like Jo did. Me. You can stay with me any time. All the time if you want. There's room. Jo might have wanted it.

Louise (*to Colin*) This year has been a bastard. How you think you can swan in after a bastard of a year and just expect to waltz off with Rosa I can't conceive. I've been the one that's had to deal with everything. Practically deal with it all. It's meant cooking food for someone who won't eat. It's been me persuading them to eat. It's been them refusing. It's been me persuading and persuading. It's been me looking at bodies and saying 'no'. Looking at dead people from the sea who aren't Jo. It's been me lying awake at night just in case I can hear someone crying. Try persuading someone of the value of regular school attendance when their life's just fallen apart. That's real. That's coping. Coping isn't some noble but ineffectual boycott, it's real bloody hard life and sometimes I've drunk coffee to keep me going. Rosa may not have been in a position to choose if it wasn't for that.

Colin It's Rosa's choice.

Pause. Dogboy whines.

He's whining.

Louise He's fine.

He whines again.

Colin Why is he making that noise?

Louise That is no concern of yours.

Dogboy barks.

Colin He just barked. (*Pause.*) Don't you think that's a little unusual?

Louise Spare me the analysis.

Colin approaches Dogboy. Louise attempts to divert him.

He's my cousin.

Colin stops.

Colin Is he?

Louise Yes. He is. He's my cousin and I'm dealing with this. So please just go and leave him alone.

Colin draws back the blanket.

Colin Where are his clothes?

Louise I've no idea. He appears to have mislaid them.

Colin Mislaid his clothes? His hands are tied. Why's that?

Louise That is absolutely none of your business.

Colin Do you treat all your relatives like this?

Louise Don't be ridiculous.

Colin Did you tie him up?

Louise Is that an accusation?

Colin Probably.

Louise We took the decision. He walked in here last night unexpectedly. He was deranged. We gave him a floor for the night. I wasn't prepared to take any risks. He was carrying a weapon. A sharp stone. It might not have been an ideal solution but it's not worked out too badly.

Colin Ideal?

Louise I'm afraid there were no rule books to consult on this one. No boycott sprung to mind. No doubt you would have proposed revolutionary socialism but unfortunately you were unable to be with us yesterday.

Colin I don't think binding a man hand and foot can be considered a solution.

Louise This happens to be the real world not a fairy tale. I don't know why you're complaining. Communism's done much worse things.

Colin I don't think communism proposes the ritual humiliation of the proletariat.

Louise The proletariat! I wondered how long it would be before you dragged them into it.

Colin Have you got something against the proletariat?

Louise I might have if they existed.

Colin This was Jo's house, Rosa. There's a neofascist spouting on about the working classes. There's a man tied up on the floor. It's like poison. You can't stay here.

Louise Poison. You're poison. Your words are poison. Jo was the sort who swallowed poison. She festered away down here, dreaming. Avoiding life. Waiting for the world to start turning her way. Only it never did. She suckled off stupid words like proletariat and the people and the vanguard and the struggle and it just drained the life out of her. The real life.

Colin What do you know about real life? You don't even smell real? You're smothered in perfume. Your life's a farce. There's a whole great suffering world out there hungry for solutions and what do you do? Double lock your front door and hope it goes away. Collaborate. Write daft articles for some pathetic publication that celebrates the female orgasm and recommends underwater mascara. Still, you don't have to worry about what's real, do you? You can just make it up as you go along. That's a luxury you can afford. You don't have to pick coffee for 60p a week. And if real life got too close for comfort, you could always crack open a decent bottle of wine and forget it. As long as I'm all right. That's the way it goes, isn't it? What's so pathetic about all this is your attempt to claim some sort of moral high ground. That's what stinks. Jo wouldn't have wanted this for you, Rosa.

Rosa Jo? Jo shouldn't have drowned.

Colin You don't want to stay here.

Louise Yes she does. Rosa wants to stay with me. Don't you? (*Pause.*) If Jo wanted the best for Rosa she wouldn't have taken her own life.

Rosa You think she took it.

Colin It was an accident.

Louise She took it because of words. Words she lived on. But what happens when the words disappear? I know what it's like to have something taken away. Something taken away and nothing put in its place. That's what people like you do. That's what Jo did to me. I know what it's like to want to pray and know there's nothing there because Jo made sure I knew. I was in pain and there was blood and I knew there was nothing. But then her words slipped away too and I was glad because then she knew what it was like. The proletariat never rounded the corner waving their flags did they? They opted for washing machines and regular supplies of eggs. And who can blame them? Because those things are real. All those people in dull, ideologically correct Eastern European places who couldn't buy toilet paper didn't stay conveniently behind the words you liked. And the words fell to the side like dead weights and your nightmare started. Well, I could live with mine, but Jo couldn't live with hers. So she died.

Colin It was an accident. Not deliberate.

Rosa She took the blue towel. She said she'd be fifteen minutes. She shouldn't have said she'd be fifteen minutes.

Louise puts her arm around Rosa.

Louise I know.

Rosa Water went in her mouth. In her eyes. She did that.

Colin It wasn't like that.

Rosa I'm glad it went in her mouth.

Colin People swimming, it happens. Cramps, currents. It happens with surprising regularity.

Louise Oh come on. Jo knew what she was doing.

Rosa She shouldn't have said it.

Colin Jo was stubborn. She never gave up on anything. She didn't see the point in giving up, stopping. You see it was me, me that always gave up on things. Not Jo. Jo used to say I let things get to my bones. That I'd let them sink too far. That I was sick with it. She'd never let things sink.

Louise I think you'd better go. Rosa's made a decision to stay with me.

Pause.

Colin (*to Dogboy*) What about you?

Dogboy I like this room. I like the way it smells.

Colin laughs.

Colin Jo used to joke. About me and trees. You're a bit of dead wood selling trees. It was a joke. But look, Rosa, look. It's no joke. I was right. Things are dead. Hell is coming. When people left those words behind things started slipping. Slipping into the sea. One of your relatives is bound hand and foot on the living room carpet and he fucking likes it. Because without those words people swallow shit. Jo went just in time. And Jo was wrong. Sometimes there is no point in trying. No point because things have slipped too far. And you know what? The lot of you get what you bloody deserve. (*Pause.*) Goodbye, Rosa. (*He exits.*)

Rosa Lectures. He always gave lectures.

Louise Jo's gone.

Rosa Yes.

Louise You're with me now. I won't desert you.

Louise hugs Rosa. Dogboy whines.

SCENE THIRTEEN

The house.
Rosa and Dogboy. Dogboy as before. Rosa is sitting still on the sofa. Dogboy edges closer to her. He rubs his head against her leg. Makes a soft growl.

Rosa What?

Dogboy sits in a begging attitude.

What do you want?

He pants.

I said I wouldn't.

He whines.

All right then.

Dogboy pants enthusiastically. She unties his hands. She immediately unties his feet. He is free. He's excited. He bounds about.

You're showing off all your bits.

Dogboy *Pardonnez-moi.* (*Pause. He pulls the blanket round him.*) I threw my clothes into the sea.

Rosa Why did you do that?

Dogboy I dunno. It was there.

Rosa It's a good thing not everyone's like you. We'd all be running round naked.

Dogboy Being naked. It's natural. It's an instinct. Dogs have instincts and they act on them. Quick. Pow. Like that. That's how they get by. They don't have thoughts. People love them. They love a dog's big furry face, its wet mouth, the way saliva suspension bridges between its teeth, the noise its paws make on lino. And their bark. A dog's bark keeps things away. Right away. It keeps things away. That's the point.

Rosa How can it?

Dogboy Come here.

Rosa Why?

Dogboy Come on?

She approaches. He growls. She slows her approach. He barks fiercely. She stops.

See.

Rosa Stupid. We used to play this game.

Dogboy listens to Rosa.

You look at someone. (*She looks at Dogboy.*) You look at them hard and then you close your eyes. (*She closes her eyes.*) You count to ten. (*She counts silently.*) And then you open them. (*She opens her eyes.*) And you see if the face you have in your head is exactly the same as the one that's in front of you. (*She looks at Dogboy.*) It never is.

Something is always different. Something, that means you can never know anything for sure. Nothing. But you have to keep looking because otherwise there's no chance of almost knowing something. The point of the game is not to stop looking. (*Pause.*) It doesn't work when the other person's gone. She never thought of that. When someone's gone it's hard to remember anything. She had a chipped tooth here. (*She indicates.*) I'll forget that soon. I'm glad. You don't need a bark to keep things away. Things go away on their own. Everything does. That's the point.

> *Pause. He sniffs. He makes a sharp move towards the sofa. Pulls out Jo's old dressing gown from beneath the covers.*

Dogboy What's that?

Rosa (*snatching it back*) It's mine. (*Pause.*) I saved it. I didn't burn it. (*Pause.*) I might need it. For the hospital later. (*She puts it on.*) See. (*She pulls it out at the stomach to demonstrate it fitting a pregnant woman.*)

Dogboy It's quite nice. (*Pause.*) I itch. I long for a good scratch.

Rosa Was it me? (*Pause.*) That did it to you. That made you like that.

Dogboy Like what?

Rosa Like you are.

Dogboy What do you mean?

> *Pause.*

Rosa You're not a dog.

Dogboy I wasn't born a dog, no. But something entered me. Something with teeth, fur and bone. I've never been so happy. (*Pause.*) Fur is itchy. Sometimes I feel like I'm on fire with it.

Rosa You could roll on the floor. That's what dogs do.

Dogboy Dogs rub against things, that's our nature. (*He begins to rub himself against the furniture.*)

Rosa watches.

Rosa Dirty old dog.

She joins in. They move over the furniture doing this. Dogboy makes small noises of appreciation.
Tony and Louise enter. Tony and Louise watch momentarily. Rosa stops.

He was whining. I let him go.

Louise Tony's got some clothes.

Tony places them on the sofa.

Tony There you are. Some clothes.

The clothes consist of plimsolls, overalls and an old white shirt.

Louise (*to Dogboy*) Perhaps you'd better put them on.

Dogboy gets up. Drops the blanket. Tony picks it up and tries to use it as a curtain. Louise looks away. Dogboy puts on the overalls.

Tony Not a bad fit.

Dogboy puts on the plimsolls.

Rosa They're too big.

Dogboy puts on the shirt. Examines his new clothes.

Louise Give him a tenner, Tony.

Tony A tenner?

Louise He may need it.

Tony What for?

Louise A bus or something.

Tony He's not getting a bus.

Louise He's not staying here.

Tony I should imagine he is. For a bit.

Louise That's out of the question, Tony.

Tony What is?

Louise He's not staying another night.

Tony Why not?

Louise Because if he does he may have even greater expectations of our assistance.

Tony He could hardly have greater expectations. He spent the night tied up.

Louise Yes. And you were the one that tied him up.

Tony Under your instructions.

Louise I didn't hold a gun to your head.

Tony Not a gun exactly. (*Pause.*) I think we should all have some breakfast.

Louise You can't go around helping people in a limp fashion, Tony.

Tony A limp fashion?

Louise Do-gooding. It just makes things worse. Unless you want to form some kind of permanent relationship with this young man, some sort of long-term relationship, then I'm suggesting that your suggestion is more cruel than kind.

Tony You're blowing this out of all proportion, Louise.

Louise There's no need to raise your voice. (*Pause.*) I'm just looking clearly at the implications of your actions. It may be fun for a night or two but I'm talking about for ever and if you can't face for ever then I'd say you were being deeply irresponsible.

Tony What sort of world would it be if we didn't hold out a helping hand to one another occasionally?

Louise We did hold out a helping hand. That was yesterday.

Tony Well, maybe that wasn't enough.

Louise Enough for what?

Tony For him.

Louise And what is enough for him? We are not his parents, Tony. There's nothing we can do. Putting him up one more night is a drop in the ocean. It's not caring, it's pretending to care. The less we pretend to care the better.

Tony I care.

Louise Tony is intent on repeating last night's fiasco indefinitely, Rosa. It seems he got some sort of kick out of it.

Tony I did not get a kick out of it. (*Pause.*) What you seem to forget, Louise, is the inestimable value of the human creature. Quite simply we must provide opportunities for that value to express itself.

Louise Ask him about his stone.

Tony His stone?

Louise Why he carries a sharpened stone.

Tony I'm sure there's a perfectly reasonable explanation. Maybe it's a lucky stone.

Louise For God's sake. Ask him. The stone.

Tony In time. In time. I can't just blurt it out. (*He goes over to Dogboy. Pause.*) Well. (*Pause.*) Ha. (*Pause.*) I was wondering. Do you always have a stone? A stone about your person.

Dogboy Not always.

Tony I see. You just like the look of this one.

Dogboy It's sharp.

Tony But you wouldn't want to hurt anyone with it?

Dogboy I could. I could hurt someone.

Tony But you wouldn't want to. You wouldn't like to hurt them?

Dogboy Yes. I would. Some people.

Tony But you'd stop yourself. You'd stop yourself when you realized it was a real live human being. With feelings.

Dogboy It might be an animal.

Tony Yes. Yes. It might be an animal.

Dogboy In the old days that's what they had stones for. For cutting at the neck.

Tony Cutting at the neck?

Dogboy takes his stone and holds it to Tony's neck. Tony is visibly startled.

Dogboy It works. I tried it. (*Pause.*) I had a dog. I had it and I cut it at the neck. I wouldn't have done it if it hadn't got on my nerves. It made a noise.

Tony Oh.

Dogboy It made a noise and it was like the noise was

142

coming from inside me. It got on my nerves. (*He takes the stone away from Tony's neck.*) That was a fucking good dog too. She had a nice lick.

Tony moves away.

Louise See. See.

Tony Don't over-react, Louise. It was a dog. Not a person.

Louise I want him out. I'm sick of useless spouted ideals. They don't help anyone. They destroy things.

Tony Just calm down.

Louise Did you hear me?

Tony I'm sorry. I'm not prepared to stand down on this one.

Louise You're not?

Pause.

Tony No.

Louise Then I'm phoning the police. They can remove him.

Tony Don't do that.

Louise This is my house.

Tony I'm perfectly aware of that.

Rosa It's my house too.

Louise Yes darling, I know.

Tony Maybe Rosa wants him to stay.

Louise She doesn't.

Tony They were playing a game when we came in.

Louise I think I'd know if they were friends.

Tony They seemed quite close.

Louise Close! What are you insinuating? I think Rosa can do better than an insane tramp.

Tony He's right there. Louise! (*Pause.*) Perhaps it was the sort of thing Rosa was used to. People staying. When Jo was here.

Louise Don't dare drag Jo into this.

Tony I'm just saying . . .

Louise What are you saying?

Tony That whatever criticisms you may make of Jo she did have room for a notion of altruism.

Louise Altruism. Do you think Jo did what she did out of altruism? Endless committees, secondary picketing, pinning nappies to the wire at Greenham. She did it because she liked the idea of telling people how to live. Because she liked the sound of her own voice, that's why she did it.

Tony Well, we don't know. She isn't here to speak for herself.

Louise No, she's got you to chirp up for her.

Tony We're only talking about one night, Louise. Actions like that they may be small but they're important. They may change something. I write books, it's the same thing. If I think those books go some small way towards changing something then I'm proud of that.

Louise Fiction never changed the face of world history, Tony, neither did the odd meagre act of selflessness. Do you know how much it takes to change something? Have you any idea of the enormity of such an enterprise? Why do you think people are satisfied with giving a little here and a little there? Why don't they give more? Everything? Because deep down inside they know it's like throwing yourself into a bottomless pit. Because there's never enough you can do. That's what people know instinctively inside them. It's not selfishness. It's realism, survival. It's the people with the guts to face up to what they've got here and now, what's in their grasp. They're the people who have joy, they're the people who have normal decent lives. They're not hiding in useless dreams or compromising their intelligence with half-baked acts of atonement.

Tony It is not half-baked.

Louise It's all or nothing, Tony. If you take him on, you take him on full stop. There won't be much time for writing. You'll need to bath him, he stinks. You'll need to find out what he eats. Cook it. Be his therapist. Mop up his piss from the toilet seat. Don't expect me to do it for you. I don't want him interfering in my normal decent life in any way. And if he touches a hair on Rosa's head I'll kill you I swear. That's the deal.

Tony You've lost your sense of perspective on this, Louise.

Louise There are fifty-two weekends a year and you're just about to give up every one of them. A thoroughly decent act of altruism I must say. I imagine your contribution to the great post-modern novel will be the first thing on the list of sacrifices.

Pause.

Tony I'm only talking about getting him on his feet, Louise. He'll have friends somewhere. Somewhere to return to.

Louise Will he?

Tony Naturally.

Rosa He hasn't any friends. He's not very popular.

Tony Usually, usually most people have friends somewhere, Rosa. Statistically he's likely to have friends.

Louise Well no one's been clamouring at our door to find him so far. It's up to you. All or nothing.

Tony I think you're being a bit extreme. About the writing.

Louise I'm being practical.

Pause.

Tony So that's how it is?

Louise Yes. That's how it is.

Tony You want me to be responsible for turning him out.

Louise That's right.

Tony Right. (*Pause. He puts his hands into his pockets. He brings out a bunch of notes. He holds them out to Dogboy.*) Here. Take it.

Pause. Dogboy does not take it.

Take it. (*He puts the money into Dogboy's hands.*) Don't worry about paying me back. (*Pause.*) You better go. (*Pause.*) Go and see social services on Monday morning. That's tomorrow. Monday. (*Pause.*) They're in the phone book. Where's the phone book, Louise?

Louise gets up and rifles through the phone book.

If I were you I'd go to them first thing. Throw your weight about. Demand to see the manager. (*He gives a short laugh.*)

Louise (*reading*) 060273. (*She tears the page out and gives it to Tony who gives it to Dogboy.*)

146

Pause.

Dogboy Gull.

Tony Pardon?

Dogboy Smell gull.

Tony Oh yes. I expect you'll remember someone. Some old friend.

Dogboy doesn't move.

He's not moving, Louise.

Louise I can see that, Tony.

*Dogboy pulls out his stone. This alerts everyone.
They are all standing.*

Tony He's got that stone again.

Louise We'll phone the police if you don't go quietly.

Dogboy barks.

Louise Jesus.

Rosa He doesn't want to go.

Dogboy barks.

Louise He knows he's got to go. Tell him.

Tony Go on, mate.

Louise Don't be over forceful, Tony.

Tony I'm sure if we all behave reasonably we can achieve a satisfactory resolution.

Louise Little bastard.

*Dogboy barks. He backs himself against a wall holding
out his stone.*

Tony He's tucked himself into a bit of a corner there, Louise.

Louise (*to Dogboy*) Just get out!

Dogboy barks.

Rosa You're making things worse.

Louise Things can't get any worse.

Rosa Much worse. (*to Dogboy*) Why don't you go!

Dogboy suddenly goes.

Louise I have to do what I think is best.

Rosa You're fucking making things worse. (*Pause.*) Will he be all right?

Tony He's been all right up to now.

Rosa So he will be all right.

Tony Yes. I expect so.

Rosa He left his coat on the beach. Do you expect he'll find that?

Louise I should think so. (*Pause.*) What do you want to do? Because if you want him to live here I won't stop you. I'll go back to London with Tony, now, immediately. You can stay here as long as you like. For ever. Like Jo did. I don't know who'll look after you. I suppose you'll look after yourself. I looked after you like a daughter. (*Pause.*)

Rosa does not move.

Rosa, why are you wearing that old thing?

Rosa What?

Louise That.

Rosa takes off the dressing gown.

That's better.

Denise enters. She is carrying a large rucksack. She has changed back into jeans, etc.

Denise This is about to split at the seams. You never know how much stuff you've got till you stick it all into a rucksack, do you? (*Pause.*) I'm off. I'm off. I've decided on the monks. Lovely calm spiritual bald monks. I knew this woman that went to Tibet and she had lunch with some. Well, she sat at their table and they included her. That's a very rare happening because on the whole monks think women are an unnecessary distraction. Like socks. (*Pause.*) I just decided. Why wait any longer? Why not go now? Instantly. Life's short. (*Pause.*) I hate men. Not you, Tony. Men like Colin. I thought his hair was ginger but it wasn't, it was sandy, like sand. I like travelling. When you're travelling you feel you're going somewhere terrific. Things go by so fast they disappear. Travelling is better than drinking and it's good for your health. This is my going away jumper. I've been saving it. Saving it for today. (*Pause.*) I've saved it so long that I've gone off it. I hate it when that happens. Still, I might like it again tomorrow. Do you like it?

Louise It's very nice.

Denise I wish I was a lesbian. That's what I wish. I'd save myself a lot of trouble. I'm going now. I hate goodbyes. Saying goodbyes. Don't say anything. I'm just going. Going now. I'm going to walk to the station. Walk by the sea. That'll be nice. Rosa, keep doing it to the power of seventeen. Don't anyone say anything. It's unlucky.

Silence. She picks up her rucksack. Goes.
   Pause.

Louise What a dreadful jumper.

SCENE FOURTEEN

Rosa on the beach. Dogboy is lying face down, curled up on the sand. Rosa looks at him.

Rosa I knew you wouldn't get far. I knew it. You're right back where you started. (*Pause. She approaches him. He doesn't move. She sees he has the stone in his hand. She prises it out.*) Let me have a go. A go holding it. (*Pause. She looks at the stone.*) Blood. (*She investigates closer. She puts her hand up to his throat which we cannot see. She draws it back and examines it. It is bloody.*) I would have come. You don't know anything do you. (*Pause.*) It's grey today, the sea. (*Pause. She begins slowly to cover him in sand.*) Some people spend time wondering what sort of mouth theirs will have. Or nose. Or eyes. They imagine the best features of themselves and their partners combined. They think what a good-looking child that would make. Only often that particular combination of features produces an extremely ugly child. A right dog. There's no rules for it. (*Pause. She continues to cover him.*) You won't need a straw. (*She stops when he is well covered. She holds the stone in her hand.*) No rules for it. (*She begins to hit herself repeatedly low down on her stomach with the hand in which she holds the stone.*) No rules for it. (*She crouches over.*)

SCENE FIFTEEN

The house. Tony and Louise.

Tony I had this thought today. I remembered this story. There's this magician and one day he goes out. And while he's out someone comes in. They come in and steal his book of spells. When the magician returns and discovers his book is missing he goes ape-shit. Suddenly he's just an ordinary guy in wacky clothes. He can't weave his magic. I remembered that today. (*Pause.*) Then I was thinking about the last thing my father said to me before he died, 'Please ensure these beds are made with corner tucks'. He used to be in the hotel trade. He believed in giving people good service. He didn't think any book of mine would do that. 'A refreshing look at famine'. That's what the *Sunday Times* said. (*Pause.*) You need people to believe in you. You need that in order to carry on.

Pause.

Louise The things I said. About your book. I never meant anything bad. You knew that, didn't you?

Tony Yes. Yes, I knew. (*Pause.*) You still have faith in me?

Louise Yes. Yes.

Tony Good. (*Pause. He touches Louise's hair. Looks at her.*) We've had quite a weekend.

Louise smiles. Puts her feet up.

On the beach.

Rosa There's blood. Where's it coming from? There's no rules. I did it just like you. Just like you. There's no rules. (*She sits still.*)

In the house.

Louise God. I'm exhausted. I'm just glad it's over.

Tony Poor Louise. You need to sleep.

Louise It is over?

Tony Don't worry. Hush hush. Louise needs to sleep.

On the beach.

Rosa I did it just like you.

In the house.

Louise This sofa could be a raft. If we keep our feet tucked up here they won't get wet. It doesn't matter how high the sea rises or how fierce the storm gets, we're safe here. Safe. Hidden. Safe.

Tony Hush. Hush.

On the beach.
  Denise enters.

Denise Rosa? It's me. Denise. I've been wandering. Wandering. I never got to the station. I've gone off Tibet. I've gone off travelling. I looked in my book. It said 'The man with the scarlet knee bands is coming'. Brilliant, I thought. (*Pause.*) I can't really think of anything to do. What shall I do?

Pause. Rosa stays looking at the sea.

Rosa Jo? Mum. Jo?

She stands up shakily.
  Lights down.

PLAYHOUSE CREATURES

Characters

Doll
Nell
Mrs Farley
The Earl of Rochester
Otway
Mrs Marshall
Mrs Betterton
Mrs Barry

Playhouse Creatures was first performed at the Old Vic
Theatre, London, on 5 September 1997 with the
following cast:

Doll Common Liz Smith
Nell Gwyn Jo Macinnes
Mrs Farley Saskia Reeves
The Earl of Rochester Dominic Rowan
Otway Steven Noonan
Mrs Marshall Rachel Power
Mrs Betterton Sheila Gish
Mrs Barry Ali White

Directed by Lynne Parker

Prologue

Doll Common enters. She is sixty or so. She seems a
vagrant, timeless. She warms her hands at a small fire. She
addresses the audience.

Doll It is a fact that I was born. That is a fact. The how
was in that old eternal way, but the when I shall not
divulge. No I'll keep that hugged close to my chest like a
sick cat. (*Pause.*) Once this was a playhouse, and before
that, a bear pit. On a hot day, I swear you could still smell
the bears. They used to rag me. 'That ain't the bears, Doll,
that's the gentlemen!' But it was bears because upon
occasion as I swept I came upon their hair. Tufts of it
bunched up in corners which I saved. As a small child, my
father was the bear keeper. I remember the bears moaning
at night, and licking the wounds at their throats where the
irons cut in and sighing, for while bears love to dance
they hate to do it for a whip. Indeed, under those
conditions, I believed they preferred fighting to the
dancing, even as blood was spilt and death faced.
Sometimes I still hear their cries very faint and in the
wind. (*She stops and listens.*)

Act One

Nell (*off*) Doll? Doll?

Nell Gwyn enters.

Is that you, Doll? I'm cold. I swear I've never been so cold.

Doll laughs.

It ain't funny, Doll. Let's have a bit of your fire. (*She muscles in.*)

Doll You ain't changed.

Nell I fancy something. I fancy hot chocolate. Warm and frothy in a silver cup.

Doll There ain't none here, your ladyship.

Nell I'll ring a bell.

Doll There ain't no bell.

Nell No bell? How do you change the scenes then?

Doll You're slow, ain't you?

Nell looks about her.

Nell This is an odd place. (*Pause.*) It's dark. Dark and it stinks. (*Pause. Nell gives a cry.*) No, Doll, no!

Doll (*mimicking*) Oh no, Doll, no.

Nell Aren't I at rest, then?

Doll begins to recite, as a taunt, as a reminder.

Doll 'Our play we perform for you this night
    For no greater cause than your delight.'

Nell This is a dream. One where I forget me lines.

Doll 'We ask alone but one small favour
    That you critics have some sweet flavour
    'Cos heaven be praised 'tis not so wise an age
    But that your own follies may supply the stage.' (*She
    does a little dance.*)

Nell Stop it, Doll, stop it.

   Doll laughs.

We need a priest, Doll. A priest!

   Doll rings a small bell she has about her.

You had a bell, you bleedin' liar!

Doll A priest! (*She exits.*)

   Nell runs after her and exits.

*A tavern scene. Outside the Cock and Pie. Two men the
worse for drink sit outside. A young woman, soberly
dressed, preaches to the unimpressed.*

Mrs Farley And lo, it is written in our Lord's book
    That this time shall come to pass,
    And ye have only to look about ye and ye will see
    That it has come to pass
    Yes, it hath.

   A burp from one of the men.
      *Nell enters from the tavern. She mops up the table
   with a cloth, collects tankards.*

Nell (*calling in*) All right! All right! In a bleedin'
minute!

Mrs Farley Brothers and sisters, you have taken the royal serpent to your bosom and there it suckles.

Wit Long live the King.

She sighs in exasperation as he passes out.

Nell These benches are for clientele that wish to purchase strong liquor. If you want to pass out do it in the gutter.

She shakes him. The wit comes round.

Mrs Farley The stink of brothel and ale house, corrupts our air and now the theatre adds its pestilential odour. All is filth, smut and scandalous entertainment.

Wit Sounds sensational. 'Nother drink.

He catches hold of Nell's skirt. With her hands full she can't pull free immediately.

Mrs Farley Ye shall see that the cows do not give sweet milk
But are dry except for stinking curdles.

Wit is sick over Nell's skirt.

Nell Ugh!

Mrs Farley Ye shall find all men to be cheats and their hair to be lice riddled. Yeah, ye shall discover even the women at your hearth to be fornicators!

Nell Fucking hell.

Wit Sorry.

Mrs Farley And a great plague of locusts will settle in the fields and pester your cows.

Nell Give it a rest!

Mrs Farley stops and begins to cry.

Nell wipes her skirt with the cloth.

What's the matter?

Mrs Farley Usually I take round the hat. Just then I was making it up. Could you tell?

Nell Seemed all right. I weren't really listening.

Mrs Farley He was my dad, the preacher. Then last week the boils came up, purple, behind his knees. Plague. This morning I thought I better just carry on. This was one of our spots.

Otway interrupts their conversation.

Otway My dad was a transvestite. He lost his job when your lot closed down the theatres. Never worked again. Starved to death. An aunt brought me up in the country. (*He fishes around in his jacket. Pulls out a tiara.*) This was his tiara. (*He puts it on.*)

Wit Terrific.

Mrs Farley I better get on. There's a lot of work to be done stamping out decadence.

Nell How much did you get today then? Stamping?

Mrs Farley Nothing. What am I going to do? I could starve. God was supposed to take care of me. But so far he's forgotten.

Nell You don't know how to work a crowd, that's your problem. I sold oysters with me sister once. We had a patter. Crowds like patter. You know 'Oyster sucking is better than . . .'

Mrs Farley We spread God's plain and holy word.

Nell It's like you have to have a bit of cunning. To get what you want.

Mrs Farley I'm not sure. I think cunning is against my religion. Well, I better go.

Nell Where?

Mrs Farley It's four o'clock. That's when I used to wash my dad's collars.

Nell No point washing 'em now. You never did like washing 'em, did you?

Mrs Farley No. It's only I can't think what else to do.

Otway I don't know what to do myself either. I'm at a loss. I saved my dad's things. I wanted to follow in his footsteps only they don't want blokes at the playhouse any more, they want ladies.

Nell Ladies?

Wit They don't take so long shaving.

Otway They turn up, show their legs and say a poem.

Wit Fantastic girls.

Otway Dad must be turning in his grave. You should see them, queening about in gold lace.

Nell Gold lace!

Otway Up close it's very tatty. Candle light lends it borrowed splendour.

Nell Do you know any poetry? I'll give you sixpence if you teach me a bit of poetry.

Mrs Farley Poetry?

Nell Can you say it?

Mrs Farley The angel of the Lord came down and glory shone around.

Nell Brilliant.

Mrs Farley Why do you want to know poetry?

Nell For a job at the playhouse.

Mrs Farley That den of defilement! That pit of pestilence!

Nell Didn't you hear? They've got lovely dresses!

Mrs Farley Do they fornicate?

Nell Fuck knows. They speak poetry and walk about.
'Oysters, oysters, by the shell or by the cup.
Slide 'em down your gullet to keep your pecker up.'

Otway How common.

Nell How many ladies do they need?

Otway They might want one more.

Mrs Farley Oh. Just one.

Nell It's my opportunity.

Mrs Farley I know an excellent poem. I have it in a book of poems at my lodgings. I'll go and fetch it.

Nell What's it called?

Mrs Farley 'The Pickle'.

Nell I'll come with you.

Mrs Farley No, it's not far. You wait. I'll meet you back here.

Nell I'll wait then. Here, I don't know your name.

Mrs Farley Elizabeth, Elizabeth Farley.

Nell And I'm Nellie. Nellie Gwyn.

Mrs Farley exits.

(*calling in*) You can stuff your poxy job. They want a lady. Lady Nell. Oysters, oysters . . . and glory shone around.

Wit A poem entitled 'The Pickle'.

Otway I'm ever so long and green and spicy.

Wit I live in a jar whip me out in a tricey.
I'm long and I'm hard and the ladies enjoy me.

Otway It only costs a half pence to employ me.

The men laugh.

Wit We didn't think you were the soft sort.

Nell I ain't.

Otway She'll be at the playhouse by now.

Nell Cunning cow. I've been bleedin' had! (*She runs off.*)

Otway Do you think I may have a talent for it? Poetry?

They exit.

Doll enters.

Doll (*addressing the audience*) I wouldn't be a liar if I told you this place used to be packed to the nines. They all sat squashed on benches, which greatly facilitated the wandering of hands down breeches and bodices. Often the talk was like the roar of water and drowned out the stage. In winter you froze and in summer you cooked. It was a foul place really, but the punters came back time after time, louts and lords, lords and louts; who could tell the difference? Not so long back they burned these places to the ground and pissed on the ashes. They swore they'd seen the last of them. But they sprung up again. Like mushrooms.

Nell enters.

Nell (*singing*) Sixpence each.
　Will you be enticed?
　Round and juicy.
　Cheap at the price.

Doll It was a moral cesspit.

Nell Oranges, I'm talking about oranges. (*She produces some oranges.*) Anything I get over the sixpence I keep for myself. I get tips 'cos of my song. I made it up.

Doll I don't like it.

Nell What's the play today?

Doll *The Fatal Maiden.* Or something or other. (*She goes off*).

Nell (*rapturously*) *The Fatal Maiden!*

The lights come up on Mrs Farley tied to a tree. She has been 'despoiled'. She is still dressed sumptuously in comparison to the last time we saw her. She poses, and sighs pitifully.

Mrs Farley O piteous fate, O horrid crime
　Which none can heal, not even time
　He tied me to this willowy tree
　I struggled but could not get free
　I felt the heat of loins afire
　He panted with his foul desire
　I am despoiled, so must expire!
　Ah. (*She dies*).

Mrs Betterton and Mrs Marshall enter. They are two Restoration actresses dressed as Amazons. They carry bows and arrows, which they fire simultaneously into the wings.
　Doll's cry is heard off stage.

Amazon One We have avenged you, alas, too late.

They indicate Mrs Farley. They gather round the tree. The recite a poem, taking turns.

Amazons In these wild woods we sadly gather
With our bows and shields of leather
Here we espy the sorry sight
Of our late queen whose piteous plight
Doth leave her here tied to this tree
O Penthisilea, we weep for thee
And bare our breasts after three.

They beat their breasts three times and after the third beat they bare a breast each.

For Amazons we still remain
And live without the rule of men.
Fierce warriors both we be
And will go down in history.

All And so the curtain falls at last.
On this our tragedy that's past.

They take their bows and exit. Mrs Farley is the last to go. As an actress she is transformed from the first demure sighting we had of her.

Nell Liz! Liz!

Mrs Farley enters.

Mrs Farley I'm Mrs Farley to you.

Nell Mrs Farley, then.

Mrs Farley What do you want?

Nell It's the same thing as before, Lizzie. Mrs Farley.

Mrs Farley Not that again. I've told you you've got to have the right way about you and you just haven't got it.

Nell What way?

Mrs Farley You've got to have a bit of breeding.
Elegance. Class. Dancing. You're selling oranges. What
more do you want?

Nell I hate oranges. What about me poem?

Mrs Farley You're never satisfied. That's your trouble.
My advice is to forget it. You don't want to lead a life of
disappointment, do you?

Nell I'm going to ask Mr Betterton. I'll get someone else
to tell us a poem, and I'll say that and show me legs.

Mrs Farley Mr Betterton has all the girls he needs. He
took on two last week. Extras.

Nell You never told me.

Mrs Farley He can't see everyone. Otherwise he'd spend
his whole life auditioning. It's a popular profession with
considerable advantages.

Nell I know. (*Pause.*) You don't want me to be one – an
actress.

Mrs Farley The theatre has to have some standards. If it
didn't, where would we be? Begging or starving. Now,
I've got to get on. (*Pause.*) You'll thank me one day.

Mrs Farley exits.
Nell watches her go.

Nell I fucking won't.

Nell exits.

A tableau.
Mrs Betterton appears as Shakespeare's Cleopatra. Doll
appears as slave or statue, holding a bowl. Mrs Marshall

169

appears as Charmian, Mrs Farley as Iras.

Cleopatra Give me my robe, put on my crown, I have
　　Immortal longings in me. Now no more
　　The juice of Egypt's grape shall moist this lip
　　Yare, Yare, good Iras; quick: methinks I hear
　　Antony call. I see him rouse himself
　　To praise my noble act. I hear him mock
　　The luck of Caesar, which the gods give men
　　To excuse their after wrath. Husband, I come:
　　Now to that name, my courage prove my title!
　　I am fire, and air; my other elements
　　I give to baser life. So, have you done?
　　Come then, and take the last warmth of my lips.
　　Farewell, kind Charmian, Iras, long farewell.

She kisses them. Iras falls and dies.

　　Have I the aspic in my lips? Dost fall?
　　If thou and nature can so gently part,
　　The stroke of death is as a lover's pinch,
　　Which hurts and is desired. Dost thou lie still?
　　If thus thou vanishest, thou tell'st the world
　　It is not worth leave-taking.

Charmian Dissolve, thick cloud, and rain, that I may say,
　　The gods themselves do weep!

Cleopatra This proves me base:
　　If she first meet the curled Antony
　　He'll make demand of her, and spend that kiss
　　Which is my heaven to have. Come thou mortal wretch,
　　(*to an asp which she applies to her breast*) With thy
　　sharp teeth this knot intrinsicate
　　Of life at once untie: poor venomous fool,
　　Be angry, and despatch. O, could'st thou speak,
　　That I might hear thee call great Caesar ass,
　　Unpolicied!

Charmian O eastern star!

Cleopatra Peace! Peace!
Dost thou not see my baby at my breast,
That sucks the nurse asleep?

Charmian O break, O break!

Cleopatra As sweet as balm, as soft as air, as gentle.
O Antony! Nay I will take thee too. (*She applies
another asp to her arm.*)
What should I stay . . . (*She falls and dies.*)

Charmian In this vile world? So fare thee well.
Now boast thee, death, in thy possession lies
A lass unparalleled. Downy windows, close,
And golden Phoebus never be beheld
Of eyes again so royal! Your crown's awry,
I'll mend it, and then play. (*She applies an asp.*)
O, come apace, despatch, I partly feel thee.
It is well done, and fitting for a princess
Descended of so many royal kings. (*She dies.*)

Tableau holds.
    And then Mrs Betterton takes her bow and exits.
    *Mrs Marshall and Mrs Farley take their bows. Doll
stands by. Voice shouts, 'Filthy whore!'*

Mrs Marshall (*whispering*) Did you hear that?

Mrs Farley (*whispering*) Ignore it.

Mrs Marshall (*whispering*) I'm going to say something.

Mrs Farley (*whispering*) No!

    *Mrs Marshall harangues an unseen member of the
    audience.*

Mrs Marshall Bastard! Poxy prick!

You are no gentleman!
Is there no one here who will run him through?
I've a mind to see his guts!

Mrs Farley looks aghast.

Doll Shut up.

Mrs Marshall He started it.

Doll Shut up.

Mrs Marshall Pointing at me, slandering me.

Doll I expect his lordship's a little inebriated.

Mrs Marshall He's pissed as fuck.

Doll We don't want trouble.

Mrs Farley You're making a show of yourself.

Mrs Marshall Miserable cheating impotent swine!

Doll Good evening.

Doll and Mrs Farley escort Mrs Marshall as they all exit.

Tiring Room.
  The actresses are gathered. Mrs Betterton addresses them.

Mrs Betterton First, pot.

Doll I emptied it Tuesday.

Mrs Betterton And now it is Friday. Mr Betterton's wishes are that it is to be emptied on a daily basis. He is the senior actor here and his orders come from higher up. From Mr Killegrew and beyond him King Charles the Second of England, Ireland, Scotland and the imperial conquests.

Doll What's he care about a piss pot?

Mrs Betterton Am I to be contradicted?

Doll No, ma'am.

Mrs Betterton Good. Then I will proceed with precipitation.

> *Doll picks up the pot and empties it unceremoniously just off. She almost bumps into Mrs Farley.*

Mrs Farley Careful!

Mrs Betterton (*reading*) The forthcoming season of works to be performed by the King's company in the summer of this year sixteen-sixty-three shall be as follows: Item, *Sir Fopling Flutter*, a comic drama by Mr Etherege in which a modern girl desires and achieves a husband of her own choosing. An unlikely play set in town. Item, *The Reluctant Shepherdess*, a pastoral epic of small moral dimension for which we shall hire extra ribald shepherds. Item three, four and five, *Macbeth the Murderer*, *Othello the Moor*, and *Hamlet the Ditherer* by our own Mr Shakespeare. Desdemona to be played by Mrs Marshall. Ophelia by Mrs Farley. Lady Macbeth by myself, Mrs Betterton. Mr Betterton will of course play the Thane, the Moor and in the absence of Mr Hart, The Dane. (*Pause.*) In the event of an actress failing to attend a performance, management retains the right of instant dismissal or on production of a decent excuse, confiscation of wages. And while we at the King's would wish no great catastrophe upon our rivals at the Duke's, neither will we be praying that funds be forthcoming for the repair of their roof.

All Amen.

Mrs Betterton As to the incident following our final performance of *Antony and Cleopatra*, Mr Betterton has

decreed that no more is to be said on the matter. Not a
word. Is that understood? (*Pause.*) May the muse attend us.

Mrs Betterton exits.
   The actresses wait till she goes.

Mrs Marshall Whore, he called me.

Doll It's his vengeance.

Mrs Farley Vengeance?

Mrs Marshall But it's me that should have the vengeance.

Doll Earl.

Mrs Marshall What?

Doll You often get that sort of behaviour off of an earl,
I've noticed. It's just their way. He'll keep on at you and
on at you. Like a wolf at a carcass. He'll never let up.

Mrs Farley Why was he shouting?

Mrs Marshall He used to come in here. He paid. To
watch us. Changing.

Doll Not me. I ain't taken nothing off for ten years.

Mrs Marshall Then he wanted to have me.

Doll She didn't fancy it.

Mrs Marshall He was a dog. But he persisted. So I said,
'Marry me and I'll do it.' Thinking he'd go cock his leg up
another tree.

Doll But he agreed.

Mrs Farley He agreed!

Mrs Marshall So I borrowed a costume.

Doll Desdemona, weren't it?

Mrs Marshall And I met him at a church in a small country village.

Doll Lewish-ham.

Mrs Marshall And we were married by a priest. I thought if he's fool enough to make me wife I'll take him for what I can get. So he had his night . . . and when I woke up the next morning he was gone.

Mrs Farley Gone?

Doll Scarpered.

Mrs Marshall The priest was no priest.

Doll He was a bleedin' actor.

Mrs Marshall I knew I'd seen his face.

Doll Earls, they go to any length. They got time on their hands, see.

Mrs Marshall I complained to the King. Lot of good it did.

Doll Lie low, I said.

Mrs Marshall And now I am publicly insulted.

Doll Hounded.

Pause.

Mrs Farley If I wanted to, could I borrow a costume?

They look at her.

I was just asking.

Doll He could ruin you. Keep coming here, heckling. I seen it before.

Mrs Marshall He'll get bored.

Doll Will he?

Mrs Marshall I could meet him. Talk, settle it.

Doll You got trouble.

Mrs Marshall I'll settle it.

On stage before a performance.
  Mrs Betterton enters, tended by Doll. Mrs Betterton moves centre and begins to declaim in the grand old way. She is quite terrifying.

Mrs Betterton I have given suck
  And know how tender 'tis to love the babe that milks
  me.
  I would, while it was smiling in my face
  Have plucked my nipple from its boneless gums
  And dashed its brains out had I so sworn as thou have
  done to this.

Doll Lord!

Mrs Betterton A fellow began to shake. He was in the front row there. (*She points.*) He shook from head to foot and crossed himself.

Doll It's the way your eyes burn.

Mrs Betterton Eyes are the windows to the soul. A lot of it's in the eyes. Mr Betterton swears by them.

Doll What do you want doing today?

Mrs Betterton Widow.

Doll It's the black then. I'll get the black out. I don't like to say nothing but I feel I must. Our costumes ain't what they were.

Mrs Betterton We haven't got money to cast to the four winds. This is the theatre.

Doll But Mr Betterton had a new costume delivered
Friday. With feathers.

Mrs Betterton Mr Betterton has given his life's blood to
this company, Doll Common, let me remind you.

Doll I am reminded.

Mrs Betterton Mr Betterton is entitled to a few feathers,
surely.

Doll He's entitled to a whole pillow.

Mrs Betterton Sometimes I wonder what would happen
to a person if it was taken away. That thing one gives
one's life blood for.

Doll I've never had the chance to give nothing. I'm
always the dead one under the cloak, or else I'm
sweeping.

Mrs Betterton I imagine it would be terrible, terrible.

Doll Still, I'm not complaining. What you've never had
you can't miss. Well we better fix you up.

Mrs Betterton Just another minute. (*Pause.*) Have you
ever noticed how quiet it is in here, before? It's as if the
air's resting.
  'The raven himself is hoarse
  That croaks the fatal entrance of Duncan
  Under my battlements!'

Nell enters from the shadows.

Nell I want to do that.

Doll Who's there?

Nell Will you show me? How to do it?

Doll It's orange moll. Mrs Betterton hasn't got time to
waste on the likes of you. Get going!

Nell I said a poem. (*Pause.*) I said it and Mr Betterton said I was to have a go. Saying something.

Mrs Betterton A line?

Nell Yes.

Mrs Betterton He never mentioned it to me.

Nell 'A line,' he said.

Mrs Betterton I suppose there's a few lines going.

Doll Nothing fancy.

Mrs Betterton I've only got fourteen myself. Have you any rural experience?

Nell Me mum kept a hen.

Mrs Betterton Well then, there's the lusty shepherdess.

Nell I'll take anything.

Mrs Betterton (*saying the line*)
'Here stroll I the live long day
Watching my fellows fork the hay.'

Nell Here stroll I . . .

Mrs Betterton And now I must prepare myself.

Doll Some of us have preparation to do!

Doll and Mrs Betterton go to the exit. Nell attempts her line as they are leaving. It is very flat and mumbled. It stops Mrs Betterton in her tracks.

Nell . . . the live long day.

Mrs Betterton Never underestimate the value of opening one's mouth while speaking. One may go a long way in the theatre with an open mouth.

Doll And not just in the theatre.

Nell opens her mouth, but gestures wildly.

Nell Watching my fellows fork the hay.

Mrs Betterton A word. Stillness.

Nell Stillness?

Mrs Betterton (*with stillness*)
'Here stroll I the live long day
Watching my fellows fork the hay.'

See?

Nell Oh yeah.

Mrs Betterton A simple technique which may upon occasion be used to stunning advantage. As a child I was encouraged to sit still for long periods of time. I've found that invaluable.

Nell I never sat still. I had worms.

Mrs Betterton You may also have noticed that my head was at ten to eleven.

Nell Your head?

Mrs Betterton If you imagine the stage as a clock. I shall demonstrate. (*She demonstrates putting her head in the correct positions.*) Submission is well expressed at six o'clock. Shame at twenty to seven. Despair at five past twelve; not to be confused with heavenly abandonment at midday exactly. Death by strangulation is one of the only occasions on which an actress may employ a quarter to three.

Nell I see.

Mrs Betterton The best way for an artist to improve their craft is by careful observation of a seasoned and expert colleague. You may observe me.

Nell Thank you.

Mrs Betterton Follow on. You are honoured in joining a profession of much heart and great decorum.

They move to the exit. Doll does not allow Nell to follow directly after Mrs Betterton.

Doll After me. And just remember, for every queen there are thirty friends at the banquet . . .

They exit.

The Tiring Room.
Mrs Marshall and Mrs Farley do each other's laces.

Mrs Farley I laughed and laughed and laughed. I couldn't stop laughing. He drank down a whole flask, and the rest of them beat the tables with their fists, and the noise was deafening, and then this woman came in, and you should have seen the state of her; she had a black eye and her hair was matted, and she had bare feet, and they got her to sing in front of the King; only she couldn't sing a note, and I laughed so much I cried; I don't know where they got her, off the streets – I think – and I never went home last night – I stayed away all night. What did you do?

Mrs Marshall Nothing. I sent word to the Earl of Oxford asking for a meeting. I waited in.

Mrs Farley And?

Mrs Marshall I got bored and went out. To a salon.

Mrs Farley A what?

Mrs Marshall Salon. In some very nice rooms. With interesting people; philosophers, wits, poets. You drink coffee and you talk.

Mrs Farley Talk? What about?

Mrs Marshall Ideas. Discoveries. They now know that the human heart has four separate compartments.

Mrs Farley Ugh!

Mrs Marshall It's science.

Mrs Farley What do they want you there for?

Mrs Marshall I'm an actress. They've never had one of those before. I'm a novelty. They ask me things.

Mrs Farley Ask you things?

Mrs Marshall About plays. About me. About life here. How we strut and fret our hour upon the stage. I like it there. It's the sort of place you can say anything. I've said things I never even knew I thought. And people listened.

Mrs Farley I never went home last night, I went somewhere else. And I'm going there again.

Mrs Betterton enters with Nell and Doll.
Nell stands amid the actresses.

Mrs Betterton Go ahead.

Nell I am new.

Mrs Betterton Speak up.

Nell I am new.

They look at her.

Mrs Farley You!

Mrs Betterton Engaged by Mr Betterton for a try out.

Mrs Marshall She's not on with me, is she?

Mrs Betterton (*introducing*) Mrs Marshall, Mrs Farley,

Mrs Gwyn. (*Pause.*) The latter follows on the former. It is all easily done. (*Pause.*) Well, well.

Mrs Marshall She'd better be proficient.

Noises are heard off stage.

Mrs Betterton See to that, Doll.

Doll goes over to the door.

An audience's place is in the auditorium. Goodness only knows what the attraction is back here.

Mrs Marshall One can only wonder.

Doll moves back from the door.

Doll Like flies round –

Mrs Farley (*interrupting*) A honey pot.

Doll goes over to the door.

Doll Bugger off! You're not coming in. There's ladies changing in here.

The noise surges.

You can wait 'til after and it'll cost ya.

The noise surges again.

They won't listen to me. They've no respect for a body.

Mrs Marshall goes over.

Mrs Marshall Shut up, you rollicking load of ball-driven fuckwits.

The noise stops, Mrs Marshall resumes her preparations.

Nell I got a good one. For swearing.

They all focus on her.

We had it where I used to work. (*Pause.*) Turnip bollocks.

This falls flat. They resume tasks, except for Mrs Farley.
She beckons Nell over.

Mrs Farley Come here.

Nell moves to her.

Show me your petticoat.

Nell What for?

Mrs Farley Show me.

Nell lifts up her skirt to reveal it. It's of greyish cloth.
Mrs Farley laughs.

What a rag.

Nell What's wrong with it?

Mrs Farley pulls up her skirt to reveal her petticoat.

That's beautiful.

Mrs Farley A gift. From an admirer.

Nell It's fucking beautiful.

Mrs Farley You could wear this in a palace.

Nell Yeah.

Mrs Farley points to Nell's petticoat.

Mrs Farley People don't want to pay to see that. That's
like paying to see a dishcloth. An actress has to have the
correct accoutrements. That's French.

Nell Blimey.

Mrs Farley Didn't he tell you about accoutrements at the
audition?

Nell No.

Mrs Farley He did me. Liar.

Nell What?

Mrs Farley You never had one, did you? Did you?

Nell No.

Mrs Farley You wouldn't listen to me, would you? We work hard for what we've got. We don't need amateurs to ruin it for us.

Nell I won't ruin it.

Mrs Farley You don't know what it's like – hundreds of faces looking at you. You don't know what that silence is like before you speak. The King's in today.

Nell He's not?

Mrs Farley Yes. He's come to see me. He thinks I look continental. He gave me this. (*She signals her petticoat*). I've been to the palace. There's special stairs round the back. They give you a candle and up you go. Next, I'm getting shoes.

Nell Shoes . . . Are you going to tell on me?

Mrs Farley Too late. You're on.

Mrs Marshall approaches.

Mrs Marshall (*to Nell*) You know what you have to do. Follow me on shortly. Don't muck it up. You look like a bleedin' ghost. Come on. (*Pause.*) Well, say something.

Nell Turnip bollocks.

Mrs Marshall God.

They exit.
Mrs Marshall is alone on stage, performing.

Mrs Marshall Here have I flown to this lonely forest

184

Fled shame, dishonour and a passion torrid.
Will I ever leave this wilderness?
What my fate will be I fear to guess.
My heart is beating strangely fast
Shall I find relief at last? (*She draws out a dagger.*)
This dagger I may employ to end my sorrow.
Yet pity says wait until the morrow.
For surely salvation swift may come
With the sweet and rising sun. (*An idea strikes her.*)
I shall call upon the Muses three
To aid me in my misery.

Doll, Mrs Betterton and Mrs Farley enter as Muses.

Mrs Betterton Who calls us from our heavenly nest?

Mrs Marshall 'Tis I.

Mrs Betterton Then ask what you will of the Muses three,
Of music.

Mrs Farley Dancing.

Doll And poet-ry.

Mrs Marshall My life is nothing to me now.

Mrs Betterton Do not bend beneath your woe
Seek out friendship, hope will flow.
Now look, here comes a shepherdess
She will give succour to your distress.

Nell enters. She comes closer and stares at the audience, terrified.

Mrs Marshall Good lady I have some small request
May I take shelter at your bower
And while away the cold night hour?

There is a dreadful silence. Nell gives a wail.

Mrs Betterton Alas we can no longer stay.

Sisters, away, away, away . . .

Mrs Betterton, Doll and Mrs Farley exit.

Mrs Marshall May I take shelter at your bower
And while away the cold night hour?

Nell is frozen.
  Mrs Marshall exits.
  *Nell still seems frozen. After a while she begins to
dance a jig. She gets livelier, warming to her task. The
audience warm to her. She dances off, triumphant.*

The Tiring Room.
  *Mrs Betterton, Doll and Mrs Farley enter. Mrs Marshall
enters very shortly after.*

Mrs Betterton (*scandalized*) Mrs Marshall.

Mrs Marshall I just left her out there.

Mrs Betterton Shameful!

Mrs Marshall I said my lines and waited for hers. She
just stood rooted to the spot. People shouting, hissing!
She kept doing funny things with her head.

Mrs Betterton She should of been at twenty to six.

Mrs Marshall What?

Mrs Betterton Mr Betterton has made a rare error in
choosing her.

Mrs Farley No, he hasn't.

Mrs Marshall You can hardly call her a natural.

Mrs Betterton It seems so. She has allowed personal
feelings to destroy her performance. Mr Betterton once
led the entire English army with a thorn in his foot. He

never manifested a twinge. Later I had to dig it out with a
cheese knife.

Mrs Farley He never chose her. You did.

Mrs Betterton I?

Mrs Farley She lied. She never saw him.

Mrs Betterton Never saw him? She said she was to have
a line. That is what she said. Didn't she?

Doll I took it with a pinch of salt.

Mrs Betterton I am thunderstruck. Mr Betterton!

Mrs Marshall (*to Mrs Farley*) You could have said
something.

Mrs Betterton I have gone over his head by
misadventure. Lord! Lord!

Doll And with royalty in.

Mrs Marshall It's us that look like fools.

Mrs Betterton Terrible! A line. She said.

Nell enters slowly, dazed. They all watch her.

Mrs Marshall You showed me right up, you silly cow.

Mrs Farley Beg your old job back, if you don't want to
starve.

Mrs Betterton I'm afraid you will not do.

Nell seems in a trance.

Nell I could not do it. You lot buggered off and left me.

Mrs Farley I told you, didn't I?

Nell Everything swayed as if it was wind in a forest and
people were hissing and that was like the sound of wind.

And I felt like a small thing that the wind was carrying, carrying somewhere, away, far away . . . Then a thought came into my head like a shout. It said do something and fucking hurry up about it. So I danced a little jig which I made up on the spot out of my head and slowly all the whistling, hissing, stopped and someone started to clap, and then they all clapped. Laughed and clapped.

Mrs Marshall They laughed and clapped?

Nell I felt like I had fire inside me or whisky.

Mrs Betterton A reprieve! He may even keep you.

Nell Will he?

Mrs Farley There's no accounting for taste.

Mrs Betterton All for a jig. Well, well, it has not turned out too badly.

Mrs Marshall For her. I'm sure I've appeared to greater advantage. (*to Doll*) Give us a rip. (*She takes her handkerchief from around her neck and holds it out.*) I get taken against my will in the second half.

Doll Anything to oblige.

Mrs Marshall Ta.

Sounds are heard from outside.

Doll That's what they're like, animals. (*She nods towards Nell.*) They get a sniff of it and they go wild.

Mrs Marshall I'll see to it.

Mrs Marshall exits.

Nell (*to Mrs Farley*) I did not mind the faces. I liked them. Like warm moons shining at me. And in a special box, a man in glitter, cheering.

Mrs Farley A man in glitter?

Doll The King.

Mrs Farley He couldn't have been cheering. How's my face?

Doll It's the same one you went with.

Mrs Farley Is it smudged?

Doll My eyes are bad. I can't do detail.

Mrs Marshall enters. She is covered in muck, especially her hair.

Mrs Marshall Stink! Stink!

They all stare.

In my hair. Crap from the road. Get it off me!

Mrs Farley Ugh!

Mrs Betterton This is real!

Doll (*sniffing*) Certainly.

Mrs Marshall Outside. Two men. He sent them. Bastards. Thugs. Pulled me out. 'This is from the Earl of Oxford,' they said. Then they rubbed shit into my hair. To teach me my manners. He sent them.

Nell It's all in her hair.

Mrs Marshall Get it off me!

Mrs Betterton (*to Doll*) It must be washed off.

Doll What did I say? At you and at you like a wolf!

Mrs Marshall gives a cry of frustration.
  Doll leads her away. Mrs Farley follows. They exit.

Mrs Betterton (*whispering to Nell*) Did you observe?

Nell Observe?

Mrs Betterton Her head. Half past six, child, half past six. Anger. Anger and the desire for vengeance.

The Tiring Room.
  The next day, Sunday. Mrs Betterton is rehearsing with Doll. She hands Doll her part.

Mrs Betterton I am Widow Welfed. It is a small part with quite a lot of belching. (*to Doll*) Are you ready?

Doll I'm not doing any funny voices.

Mrs Betterton I don't require any.

  Doll begins as Squire Squeamish.

Doll Good day, Widow Welfed.

Mrs Betterton Good day, Squire Squeamish. (*She belches throughout at short intervals.*) Please excuse me, it is barely past midday and I have already consumed several birds of rare plumage. The last put up quite a struggle and would not go down. Squire, Squire, you grow quite pale and seem to require salts.

Doll Salts! You would not eat me?

Mrs Betterton Do not tremble, nor rattle the door in a vain pretence of escape. I am no mere morsel! I am a red-blooded creature. Take your chance now while the servants are at market.

Doll There is a loud cry as if he has fallen from a great height. I can't do cries. I'd show myself up.

Mrs Betterton That was quite satisfactory.

Doll This is our seventh. I been counting.

Mrs Betterton Seventh?

Doll Widow.

Mrs Betterton You've no business, counting. Did you have permission to count?

Doll No. Ma'am.

Mrs Betterton No. (*Pause.*) In any case it's six. Six widows.

Doll Seven, if you count the feeble-brained spinster.

Mrs Betterton Well, I am not counting her. She is an altogether different question.

Doll When are we doing the Queen again? The Scottish one.

Mrs Betterton Soon, soon. Rest assured.

Doll I like her. She's horrible.

Mrs Betterton If I asked you a question would you give me an honest answer?

Doll Cross my heart and spit on a corpse.

Mrs Betterton Am I old?

Doll No.

Mrs Betterton Good.

Doll Not compared to me.

Mrs Betterton Mr Betterton said, 'We are getting older.' I could hardly believe he was talking to me. (*Pause. She brings out a candle.*) This is the most wonderful scene. The Queen has become a child. She sings rhymes. 'The Thane of Fife had a wife . . .' Why did she go mad, Doll?

Doll She killed a couple of geezers. It done her head in.

Mrs Betterton Could be. Could be.

Mrs Marshall enters.

Doll What you doing here? It's Sunday.

Mrs Marshall (*referring to the candle*) I need that.

Doll It's a company asset.

Mrs Marshall Give it to me.

Mrs Marshall attempts to take the candle, but Doll refuses to hand it over.

Doll Don't get vicious.

She hands over the candle. Mrs Marshall takes it and begins carving it with a small knife.

What you doing?

Mrs Marshall Nothing.

Doll Looks like nothing.

Mrs Farley enters.

Mrs Farley I didn't think there'd be anyone here.

Doll Me and Mrs Betterton have been practising. (*She refers to Mrs Marshall.*) She's taking a knife to theatrical property.

Mrs Farley begins to hunt about for bits of costume in order to add to her own for glamour's sake. She holds something up to herself, a shawl.

Mrs Betterton I hope you're not entertaining the notion of leaving this establishment attired in thespian habiliments.

Mrs Farley What?

Doll In your costume.

Mrs Betterton Mr Betterton has prohibited the wearing of such apparel outside of working hours due to the fact that they are returned lamentably besmirched.

Mrs Farley I've got a rendezvous. An extremely important rendezvous. I can't go in rags.

Doll Shall I get it off her? I have three long nails.

Mrs Betterton No, no. Such a strategy may entail further damage to company property.

Mrs Farley I'm surprised we don't go around naked on the pittance we get here.

Mrs Betterton Pecuniary considerations should hardly concern us.

Mrs Farley Why? It's not as if it's a part-time occupation. If I'm not performing, I'm learning lines. Two plays a week.

Mrs Betterton Of course. We are artists. Artists work for the love of their craft. Artists would work for nothing.

Mrs Farley Nothing!

Mrs Betterton It's a calling.

Mrs Farley You can't live on a calling. Air's the only thing that's free and you can starve on that.

Mrs Betterton People come here, high born and low. They come to our theatre to partake in the sublime. To be part of that peculiar something that uplifts and transforms. To see real actors perform.

Mrs Farley Real actors? I'm real, aren't I?

Mrs Betterton You! (*Pause.*) You are free to spend your free time as you choose. But not in our costumes. So, kindly remove them now.

Mrs Farley You can't tell me what to do.

Mrs Betterton This is tedious.

Mrs Farley They don't come to see you. They come to see us.

Mrs Betterton Us?

Doll Don't take no notice of her.

Mrs Betterton Us?

Mrs Farley The young ones. With decent legs.

Mrs Betterton Legs.

Mrs Farley They can't get enough of it. Of us. They don't even see you. Not really see. Everyone knows.

Mrs Betterton They see me. (*Pause.*) Of course they do.

Doll Don't listen to her. What does she know? Mrs Betterton has come here every day of her life. Even when it was closed down. She does exercises with her tongue, to make the words better. I seen her. I seen her up all night with lines. I seen her wash her hands a hundred times so she could say it on stage and you'd believe her.

Mrs Betterton It's all right, Doll. I am aware. I am aware there are those types. The types that come for flesh. But I am dumbstruck for you. Sorry for you.

Mrs Farley Sorry for me?

Mrs Betterton If you have not had the joy.

Mrs Farley I'm going now. There's a carriage waiting for me. I've got a rendezvous. You've probably never had one of those.

She goes to the exit. Nell enters, running.

Nell Liz!

Mrs Farley Not now. I'm late.

Nell But Liz.

Mrs Farley I can't stop now.

Nell I was told to give you this. (*She hands Mrs Farley a single coin.*) A man gave it me, to put it into your hands.

Mrs Farley A man.

Nell A messenger. He said to tell you 'parting gift'.

Mrs Farley Parting gift – and that's all he gave you. This coin?

Nell That's all.

Mrs Farley sits down.

Mrs Farley Parting gift. Are you sure that's what he said?

Nell Yes.

Pause.

Mrs Farley And that's all he gave you?

Nell Yes.

Pause. Mrs Farley is devastated.

Never mind.

Mrs Farley What do you know!

Mrs Marshall stops her carving.

Mrs Marshall There. (*She holds it up.*)

Nell What is it?

Mrs Marshall gives it to her.

Mrs Marshall Have a look.

Nell Ain't it good! A little man. A wax man.

She tries to show Mrs Farley.

Mrs Marshall Homunculus.

Nell He's got a little mouth. His mouth is open. Like a cry.

She offers it to Doll.

Doll I'm not touching it. It has hair. Melted on the top.

Mrs Marshall I had a lock of his hair. The Earl of Oxford. He gave it to me. A love token.

Mrs Betterton also looks.

Mrs Betterton Rebecca Marshall, that is evil. What are you doing now?

Mrs Marshall I'm sticking a pin in the bastard's neck.

They wince.

That is for the shit rubbed into my hair.

Nell It has gone right through!

Mrs Farley Will he feel it?

Mrs Marshall sticks another pin in.

Mrs Marshall That is for crying whore!

Mrs Betterton He will be in pain.

Doll He will be in bleedin' agony.

Another pin goes in.

Nell That's his bollocks.

Mrs Betterton It is witchery!

Mrs Marshall (*holding up the doll*)
Round about the cauldron go.

In the poison'd entrails throw.
Toad, that under cold stone
Days and nights has thirty-one
Sweltered, venom, sleeping got
Boil thou first in the charm'd pot.

Mrs Betterton Fillet of a fenny snake.
In the cauldron boil and bake.

Mrs Marshall Eye of newt and toe of frog
Wool of bat and tongue of dog.

Mrs Betterton Adder's fork and blind worm's sting.

Mrs Farley Lizard's leg and howlet's wing.

Mrs Betterton For a charm of powerful trouble
Like a hell broth boil and bubble.

Mrs Farley/Mrs Betterton/Mrs Marshall/Doll
Double double toil and trouble
Fire burn and cauldron bubble.

Nell joins in with a demonic version of her jig.

Double double toil and trouble
Fire burn and cauldron bubble.

The chant grows to a crescendo as Mrs Marshall throws the doll to the floor and tramples it underfoot.

Double double toil and trouble
Fire burn and cauldron bubble.

Mrs Marshall Never Prosper! (*She spits on it. She addresses the actresses.*) He was my keeper. Now look at him.

Mrs Farley You need a keeper.

Doll You won't get another one.

Mrs Marshall I don't want another one. I had a husband

once. You wouldn't have known me. I used to creep about. He liked me to be quiet. (*She picks up pieces of the doll and puts them in her pocket.*)

Mrs Farley I want a drink. If he don't want me. Someone else will. Won't they?

Doll 'Course.

Mrs Marshall I went out last night. To a salon. Someone remarked that he'd never known of so much interest in the theatre, not since we actresses had arrived. Could I corroborate that, he asked? Oh yes, I said. Certainly. I'll corroborate it. 'You'll be wanting to own the theatres next,' he said. 'Profits and all.' (*Pause.*) I'll have a drink too. (*to Nell*) You coming?

Nell In a bit.

Mrs Betterton I shall not be joining you. We have old friends for supper.

Mrs Betterton, Mrs Marshall and Mrs Farley exit.

Doll I fancy a bit of sweeping. (*She begins to sweep.*)

Nell I had a message, too. From the man. He said there is a carriage outside and I may use it at my own convenience. The special stairs . . . (*Pause.*) What do you think, Doll? The King.

Doll Life's like a storm, that's what I think. Don't get in its way. That's what I think. It don't matter what anyone does, we all end up dead meat, don't we?

Nell You look on the bleedin' dark side, Doll. That's your trouble. Anyway, I decided. I'll go. Just this once, mind. I'm an actress, not a tart.

Nell exits.
Doll sweeps.

As Doll exits Mrs Barry enters furtively, a young plain woman.

Mrs Barry This is where they sit. This is where they put their costumes on and take them off again and go out into the night. The smell of this place. It's heavenly! Heavenly! I just want to stand here for ever. I never want to leave. I just want to live in the corner there. Oh happy corner! Dear God please let me be an actress please, please. If I could have just this one thing. I'd give anything, anything. I know I'm not pretty. I'd tear out my heart and give it to you, God, if you just let me have this one thing. Just to be an actress. Please. Please. The world outside is grey and boring. But here, everything is different. It's magic. Magic.

She sits down dreamily.
  Curtain.

Act Two

A performance is in progress. Nell and Mrs Marshall are in breeches, sparklingly confident, each with a sword.

Nell How now, sir. You're in my path!

Mrs Marshall Nay, you are in mine, sire!

Nell I take exception to that.

Mrs Marshall And I too. Will you not step from my course?

Nell I'm buggered if I will.

Mrs Marshall Then I take you for an intolerable, plaguey rogue.

Nell And I take you for a right ambling Harry.

Mrs Marshall Will you draw, sir?

Nell Certainly.

They draw their swords.

Prepare to gasp your last.

Mrs Marshall Say farewell to the sun. *(aside)* Mind, he has a fine pair of legs for one so foul lipped.

Nell *(aside)* I swear the oaf has a mouth the colour of cherries.

They begin to fight with gusto.

Are you willing to submit to a superior striker, sirrah?

Mrs Marshall Sure it is you, Sir Feeble, who must crumble!

Nell and Mrs Marshall (*together aside*) Odd! I could swear there is something, almost womanly in the deftness, grace and expert sword wielding of this stranger.

They fight some more. They come close together, their hats fall off.

I declare!

Nell Sister!

Mrs Marshall Friend!

Nell Both disguised.

Mrs Marshall Accounting for such noble limbs and lustrous eyes.

Nell and Mrs Marshall Let us waste no time in further strife
And without delay make amends
It is far more profitable to be friends
For us women in a land of men
So let us share our victory
Enjoying our mutual company.

They turn to the audience.

And while we're at it, playing for your pleasure
We'll ask shares in your payments for good measure
The price of our glorious forms you see
Is shares in this very company.

They laugh, bow, and exit.

Mrs Betterton comes forward, and addresses Mr Betterton, who is unseen in the auditorium.

Mrs Betterton Thomas? Thomas? It is the matter we discussed at breakfast. You remember. (*Pause.*) I am afraid it has come up again. I know there is no precedent for it, dear. But in answer to that I have been told to reply that indeed there was no precedent for a wig till the first man did wear one. And now. Lo! There is scarcely a fellow who does not sport one. Bristly or fluffy. You cannot step out of doors nowadays but you see a periwig advancing towards you at great speed and in danger of toppling. (*Pause.*) Sorry, I do digress. (*Pause.*) No, my dear, we were not referring to your particular wig. How could you think so? (*Pause.*) Dear heart, they will have shares. Shares, shares, they talk nothing but shares. They say you have shares and they will have them too. Company shares and profits. (*Pause.*) You may say that they have got above themselves. What with all the fuss there is about them. Royalty and whatnot. Carriages and flowers, messages and hangers on. That may be the case. Indeed it may. But that does not alter the fact that they will not be dissuaded from their course. They say that the town does not come to see fusty old men in squashed hats declaim Caesar but to see actresses in the flesh, living and breathing, the real creatures. (*Pause*) Squashed. (*Pause.*) Yes, I explained that it was your lucky hat, my dear, passed down through the generations. (*Pause.*) I can't remember their reply to that. (*Pause.*) No! It is not that I am asking. I ask only because I am asked to ask. But still, it would seem unfair to me that the others should have shares and I none. Am I to sit in the tiring room and watch them count out their coins while I knit mittens? Why, I should not like that. Indeed no. Also, dear, we need a new cupboard for the cheeses especially, and if I have not asked you once for the means I have asked you a thousand times till I am quite worn thin with asking. And if I did have shares I should certainly know how to put the cash to good purpose. Besides, I should also like to venture a few small opinions of my own concerning artistic matters. (*Pause.*) Indeed, Thomas, you are the one that's partial to cheese. (*She exits.*)

Otway reads to the company from his new play.

Otway If kingdoms fall and princes with 'em
If the world appears a hell and not a heaven
If buns will rise but loaves refuse to leaven
Tis not this poet's fault, he's merely telling
tales of folks such as you, foolish and foul smelling
And he blames you for it, for if you were all better
He need not have lifted his pen to write a letter.

He bows, a thin smattering of applause.

Mrs Betterton Thank you, thank you Mr Otway. Indeed I have not passed four and a quarter hours more pleasantly since I can remember.

Doll I am numb all over.

Mrs Farley (*starting awake*) Are we finished?

Mrs Betterton Mr Betterton did bid me tell you that he was called away upon urgent business of a private nature. He wishes you assured he was much struck by your play; such elegance of phrase, such well modulated passion and soaring tragedy but perhaps it could be a little shorter.

Otway Shorter? Shorter? But how may that be done?

Mrs Betterton By the removal of words, Mr Otway.

Otway The removal of words?

Mrs Betterton And also lines, scenes perhaps.

Doll Acts at a push.

Otway But I need every word.

Mrs Betterton You may but we certainly do not. Have you eaten lately, Mr Otway?

Otway Not lately.

Mrs Betterton Biscuit, Doll.

Doll gives him a biscuit.

Otway Thank you, ma'am.

Mrs Betterton I shall tell Mr Betterton we have you persuaded.

Nell What's my part then?

Mrs Betterton The saintly martyred Dorothea.

Nell But she's not funny.

Mrs Betterton No, she's saintly.

Nell How do you play that?

Mrs Farley I can imagine playing it.

Mrs Betterton A prerequisite for playing any part is staying awake to hear it read.

Mrs Farley Am I the one that gets eaten by a mountain lion?

Mrs Betterton That would seem most suitable.

Nell I don't mind doing Dorothea if he takes out the saintly bits.

Mrs Betterton That would leave her somewhat skeletal. It is not for us to come between a poet and his muse. If it were I would be the first to suggest the creation of a large and diverting part for a maturer woman.

Otway I can't quite see it, myself.

Mrs Betterton We are an excellent company, Mr Otway, and have made many a play appear satisfactory as would have turned a man's stomach to have read 'em. Excuse me.

Exits.

Nell I want a few jokes.

Otway I don't quite see Dorothea like that. I see her as transcendent.

Nell Could be off after one night.

Otway My play! I don't think so.

Nell It has been known. Sometimes we forget our words.

Mrs Marshall Or we forget to come on.

Otway I'm sorry. I can't betray my talent with this brand of low bargaining.

Nell I'm not showing me tits then.

Otway I don't know what you mean.

Mrs Marshall She means her part is a tit part.

Nell And if I'm going to make a tit of myself I want a few jokes.

Otway This play is a serious indictment of primogeniture.

Nell It's tit after tit.

Mrs Marshall reads.

Mrs Marshall Marcellus spies Dorothea asleep on a grassy knoll.

Nell Tit hanging out.

Mrs Marshall Dorothea discovered praying in her boudoir.

Nell Other tit hanging out.

Mrs Marshall Vincolo struggles violently with Dorothea in the lonely cloisters.

Nell Both tits out simultaneous.

Otway All right. You can have a few jokes. They'll have to be religious.

Nell That's all right. Religion's funny.

Mrs Farley I don't mind being eaten but I'd like a proper speech. It just says ow.

Otway It's hard being a writer. There's so many people to please. Not to mention the audience. Good ideas are hard to come by I can tell you.

Mrs Marshall I've got an idea. For a tragedy. The main part is a woman.

Otway I can't see that.

Mrs Marshall Her name is . . . Monimia. She's married but she takes a lover.

Doll Tart.

Mrs Marshall She doesn't know she has. She's been tricked. She thinks it's her husband she's sleeping with but really it's his brother who's smitten with her. Should she tell her husband or live a lie?

All Live a lie / tell him.

Mrs Marshall She tells him. He is furious. She's punished, blamed. She suffers. Being an orphan she has no one to turn to.

Doll Can't you give her a cousin?

Mrs Marshall No. (*to Otway*) You give that to an actress and she wouldn't let it stop running. Think about it.

Otway No no no no no. (*Pause.*) Monimia?

They exit.

Mrs Betterton and Doll enter.

Mrs Betterton Doll? Do you ever hear things? Voices?

Doll What sort of voices?

Mrs Betterton Ethereal voices. They have told me 'The waiting will not be for much longer.'

Doll What waiting?

Mrs Betterton For a part. A great part.

Doll How do you know they're telling the truth? Voices can be tricksy.

Mrs Betterton I have proof. See this. (*She holds out her hand.*)

Doll Wedding ring.

Mrs Betterton One morning I woke up, and for the first time in thirty years it was not on my finger. They told me where to find it, and they were right.

Doll Where was it?

Mrs Betterton In the slops bucket.

Doll How'd it get in there?

Mrs Betterton I've no idea. No idea. Not to wait much longer, they said. Not much longer.

Mrs Farley enters, hurrying. She has a blanket round her.

Mrs Farley (*to Doll*) My laces, Doll. You've got to do my laces. I'm late.

Doll Patience is a virtue.

Mrs Farley (*turning her back to Doll*) Pull 'em tight, Doll.

Doll I am pulling them.

Mrs Farley That ain't tight enough.

Doll Me poor old fingers are giving out.

Mrs Farley You do it, and I'll give you threepence.

Doll Fourpence.

Mrs Farley Done.

Doll Mind. I'm not saying I can work miracles.

Mrs Marshall and Nell enter. A rehearsal.
   The following is an extract from The Provoked Wife.
*With Mrs Marshall as Lady Fanciful, Nell as
Mademoiselle, Mrs Betterton as Cornet and Mrs Farley
as Pipe.*

Lady Fanciful Cornet! Cornet!

Cornet enters.

Cornet Ma'am.

Lady Fanciful How do I look this morning?

Cornet Your ladyship looks very ill, truly.

Lady Fanciful Lard, how ill-natured thou are, Cornet, to
tell me so, though the thing should be true.

Mademoiselle My opinion pe, matam, dat your ladyship
never look so well in your life.

Lady Fanciful Well, the French are the prettiest obliging
people; they say the most acceptable, well-mannered
things, and never flatter.

Mademoiselle Ah, matam, I wish I was fine gentleman
for your sake. I'd do all de ting in de world to get a leetel
way into your heart. I make song, I make verse, I give
you de serenade, I give you great many present; I no eat,
I no sleep, I be lean, I be mad, I hang myself, I drown

myself. Ah, *ma chère dame, que je vous aimerais!*

Lady Fanciful Well, the French have strange obliging ways with 'em. You may take those two pairs of gloves, Mademoiselle.

Mademoiselle Me humbly tanke my sweet lady.

Cornet enters.

Cornet Here is Pipe, ma'am. To sing you a song.

Pause. Pipe does not enter.

Here is Pipe, ma'am. To sing you a song.

Pause.

Nell Pipe! We ain't got all day.

Mrs Farley as Pipe enters, coming forward slowly. She is now visibly pregnant. She begins to sing.

Mrs Farley Fly, fly, you happy shepherds, fly . . . (*She stops, drying up. She tries again.*) Fly, fly.

Mrs Marshall You're nothing like a pipe.

Mrs Farley I can sing, can't I?

Doll You're showing.

Mrs Farley It's not that bad.

Mrs Betterton Someone else will have to be Pipe.

Mrs Farley Who?

Mrs Betterton I expect Mr Betterton will see to it. Some new girl.

Mrs Farley I am Pipe.

Mrs Betterton You will not do. Not in your present way.

Mrs Farley I'll tie my lace tighter.

Doll You and whose army?

Mrs Farley I'm not on long. Let's get on with it. (*She sings.*) Fly, fly . . . come on!

The others return to the Tiring Room. Mrs Farley follows them.

Mrs Betterton It is impossible. Mr Betterton will not have it. He cannot. We could lose our licence. To be that way on a public stage. There are laws.

Mrs Farley Laws!

Mrs Marshall You knew about them. If we were all as careless as you, the theatre would have to close down.

Mrs Farley It's not my fault.

Mrs Marshall Whose fault is it, then?

Mrs Farley I went back looking for the special stairs but I couldn't find them. They took me there before and it was easy, but when I went back I couldn't find them. It was like a maze. I wandered and wandered. You get tired. Where will I go?

Mrs Marshall You should have thought about that.

Mrs Farley Please.

Mrs Betterton There's no choice in the matter.

Doll You've been lucky hanging on this long.

Mrs Farley turns to Mrs Marshall.

Mrs Farley Help me.

Mrs Marshall What do you mean?

Mrs Farley You know.

Doll You don't want to do that.

Mrs Farley Who asked you? (*to Mrs Marshall*) I want you to do it.

Mrs Marshall No.

Mrs Farley You've got to. Please.

Doll I knew a woman who rotted inside, after.

Nell Shut up, Doll.

Mrs Farley It's not too late, is it?

Mrs Marshall It's never too late. Have you seen it done before?

Mrs Farley No.

Mrs Betterton I've seen it done.

Mrs Marshall Sit down.

Mrs Farley sits down.

Get a cloth.

Doll gets a cloth.

Mrs Farley Is that for blood?

Mrs Marshall No. You put it in your mouth and bite on it.

Doll You need something sharp. Long and sharp.

Mrs Betterton fetches a long pin from a costume brooch.

Mrs Betterton Here. A queen's brooch.

Mrs Marshall takes it.

Mrs Marshall Give us your arm.

She takes Mrs Farley's arm. She sticks the pin into it. Mrs Farley cries out.

Mrs Farley Ah!

Mrs Marshall That's nothing. Still want it done?

Pause. Mrs Farley nods. The women close round her.

Mrs Farley Hold my hand, someone.

Nell holds her hand. They begin. Mrs Farley gives a more awful cry. Then a worse cry.

No! (*She takes the rag from her mouth.*) I can't. I can't.

The women move away from her.

Mrs Marshall It doesn't always work.

Pause.

Mrs Farley Before I go. Would any of you ladies care to purchase a petticoat? Well fashioned and stitched. It's pure silk. French. (*She lifts her skirt to show it.*) An absolutely invaluable accoutrement. (*She takes it off and holds it out.*) Well.

Mrs Betterton It's very pretty, but not to my particular taste.

Doll I'd only use it as a snot rag.

Mrs Farley It's hardly worn. What's the matter?

She waves the petticoat closer to the women; they back away so as not to be touched by it.

Superstitious? I said, 'It's hardly worn'!

Nell I'll buy it.

Nell gives her the money.

Mrs Farley Thanks. (*She offers Nell the petticoat.*)

Nell You keep it.

Mrs Farley keeps hold of it.

Mrs Marshall How long are you going to live off a petticoat?

Mrs Farley Maybe you should have a care. Maybe your luck will run out. (*She exits.*)

Mrs Marshall A petticoat never saved anyone.

Mrs Barry enters the empty Tiring Room.
A man enters. It is the wit from Scene One. The Earl of Rochester.

Rochester Are you going to take some clothes off or what?

Mrs Barry What?

Rochester Are you an actress or not?

Mrs Barry No, I'm not. (*She tries not to cry.*)

Rochester Could you take your clothes off in any case?

Mrs Barry My heart is cleft in twain.

Rochester God. Spine turned to water. Head pranging. Mouth scraped dry as death's dick. Got a drink there, girl?

Mrs Barry No moisture shall ever moist these lips.

Rochester Pass us a carafe. There's a good girl.

Mrs Barry Fists beat my breasts. Nails shred them.

Rochester Don't do that. Such nice breasts.

Mrs Barry Who are you?

Rochester Please allow me to introduce myself. I am the Earl of Rochester. Who are you?

Mrs Barry No one. I am wretched and downcast. Mr

Betterton will not take me into his company. He says I am devoid of talent and sport a droopy eye.

Rochester May I be of assistance.

Mrs Barry What can you do? I was born that way. Oh plunge your dagger between my ribs and let me fall into sulphurous eternity.

Rochester You know your problem?

Mrs Barry No.

Rochester You're histrionic. You don't do things like they do in life. In life when people want to die they say, 'Give us another drink.' Give us another drink.

Mrs Barry I don't understand.

Rochester Yes. Very nice tits. I'll teach you if you like.

Mrs Barry Teach me?

Rochester You'll be the best actress that ever breathed.

Mrs Barry How will you do that?

Rochester See that. (*He points to a play.*) Pick it up.

She does so.

It's diseased with the plague.

She screams and throws the play across the room.

Not really.

Mrs Barry I don't like you.

Rochester Now do it again. Go on do you want to be an actress or not?

She picks it up.

Do it again. Just like you did before.

214

She throws it histrionically.

No no no no. Don't demonstrate. Just remember exactly how it felt. You were holding death in your hands. There is nothing more terrible to anyone than that.

Mrs Barry Then why are you drinking yourself to death?

Rochester It's a puzzle, isn't it? Now. Go on. Remember step for step how you felt. Exactly.

This time Mrs Barry does a decent reconstruction.

Better. Better. I think we're on to something. Now you can get me a drink.

Mrs Barry The best actress that ever lived. You swear.

Rochester Absolutely. What's life without a challenge?

They exit.

The Tiring Room.

Doll I saw the old king. I saw him put his head on the block. Then whoosh.

Nell What was that like?

Doll Well, it sort of rolled off.

Mrs Betterton From today I shall not be attending the theatre on a regular basis.

Doll Gawd.

Mrs Betterton Mr Betterton has talked to me.

Doll You never said.

Mrs Betterton Some younger actresses must be given a chance. People like to see them.

Doll Gawd.

Mrs Betterton They will partner Mr Betterton. We were partners for many years. Many years. (*She sits very still and does not move.*)

Doll Mrs B? Mrs B?

Nell Mrs Betterton? Mrs Betterton?

Mrs Marshall She'll come to herself.

Mrs Betterton I used to help my husband with his lines. And naturally, I learnt them too. Then one day, he was playing Othello and his Iago fell sick. He ate something that disagreed with him. A pork pie. Anyway, it was rotten. Mr Betterton was caught short and could not find anyone else at such little notice to do the part. Except for me. I'd read it with him many times. We knew it could mean trouble if the bishops found me out, being a woman, but we were younger and reckless and we thought no one would ever know.

Nell What happened?

Mrs Betterton We got away with it. We were very close, Mr Betterton and I, and it was as if I hung off his breath, and he off mine, and the words flew between us. That was my first time. (*Pause.*) After that we did it on a regular basis. My fool to his Lear, his Falstaff to my Hal. And then, of course, the day came when everything changed and for the first time we women were permitted by Royal decree to act upon a stage. A great stir it caused. And I was one of the first ever and when I spoke, a great hush descended on the house, and it was as if the men and women gathered there were watching a miracle, like water turning to wine or a sick man coming to health. (*Pause.*) It was then I knew that I had done a terrible thing and that nothing would ever be the same for me again. I had tasted a forbidden fruit and its poisons had sunk deep into my soul. You see, Iago is like a whip that drives the life around him, when Hal makes a choice the whole world holds its breath. I never forgot that feeling. The poison's still in my blood. Like a longing. A longing. I looked for that poison everywhere and couldn't find it. Not in the Desdemonas or Ophelias. Only in her, the dark woman. (*Pause.*) We were partners for many years. And when he told me it was over, I swear he had tears in his eyes. I had never seen him cry before, except, of course, when the part required it.

Pause.

Nell You better go home, Mrs B.

Doll Better wait at home. Not here. You don't want him finding you. He'll think you've gone funny.

Mrs Betterton I've never missed a cue.

Nell We know that. We know.

Mrs Marshall You can't stay sitting here.

Mrs Betterton Then I shall approach my husband once more for tomorrow's performance. I am not above a woman selling artichokes.

Mrs Betterton exits.

Mrs Marshall The first time I was ever in a theatre I saw her. Somehow she just knew how to do things. Even the business with the bloody clocks.

Doll Fate is a wicked thing. Time don't have pity on no one. No one.

Outside the theatre some time later.
  Mrs Farley is standing alone. She looks ill, dirty,

bedraggled, weak. She is clad in her petticoat, which is dirty, ragged.

Mrs Farley Two pence. Two pence. I do anything. You can punch me. Look! (*She shows her arms, which are bruised.*) Nothing. Stood here all afternoon. Nothing doing. Should have washed my face. Tired. Too tired to do it. I might have done better business if I had. (*Pause.*) It's not me. It's them. They're not doing their job properly. The blokes aren't coming out excited. They're coming out limp. They're not coming out looking for it. I should be in there. Not outside. (*Pause.*) Thing is, I'm better now. Better than I was. That's the pity of it. I've learnt things out here. The art of performance. You can't act tired, not for business purposes. You've got to act like you like it. Love it even. You learn that. Out here I'm a real pro. (*Pause.*) I left it. Had to. Little white body. Laid it on some steps. What a cry when I left it. (*Pause.*) I'm going to find a gutter or a corner and lie down. Not in the street! Yes. Right here in the street. (*She begins to wander off.*) It's getting dark, dark.

She exits.

Tiring Room.
  Nell prepares for a rendezvous.

Doll I thought you was only going once.

Nell You're not paid to think, are you?

Doll Here's her parts. (*She shows her a bag of scrolls.*) I have to give 'em. To her.

Nell Who?

Mrs Marshall enters.

Doll (*loudly*) Her! (*She shoves the bag at Mrs Marshall.*)

Here y'are. Assorted queens and wives. Faithful have a blue star, unfaithful a red circle.

Mrs Marshall Parts?

Doll She's had 'em years. (*She drinks some more.*)

Mrs Marshall Nell, we are no longer hirelings.

Doll Starlings?

Mrs Marshall Hirelings. Hirelings. (*to Nell*) Me and you, Nell. We are shareholders.

Nell Fuck!

Mrs Marshall It has been agreed. We have shares.

Doll I thought you said 'Starlings'.

Nell Cheers. (*She takes a cup and drinks. She hands it to Mrs Marshall.*) Shareholders!

Mrs Marshall Shareholders!

They celebrate.

Nell They saw sense then. I'll drink to that tonight. (*She picks up a shawl in preparation for leaving.*)

Mrs Marshall You don't have to go now.

Nell Don't have to?

Mrs Marshall Your rendezvous.

Nell It's arranged.

Mrs Marshall Things have changed, Nell. As fast as that. The point is you can choose. That's the point. You don't have to go.

Nell I want to bloody go. (*Pause.*) It's all his hair. That hair's real. Lovely black hair.

Mrs Marshall Are you in love?

Nell Love? Going there. It's exciting. I'm sixteen. I want to try things. New things. I'm lucky. I've always been lucky. People say I'm beautiful, but so are lots of girls. So why me? Why me and the King? Luck. That's all. I get what I want. I always have. I had my own oyster stall at eleven. I have this thing I do. I imagine. I imagine what I want and then I get it. Somehow I get it. It just seems to go on and on and on. And I became an actress and I got the King.

Mrs Marshall I imagine things, too. I imagined not having a keeper. Freedom.

Nell And you got it. We're different, that's all. I'm free to do what I want, and you are too.

Mrs Marshall Free. To play a faithful wife or an unfaithful wife. A whore, a mistress. We play at being what we are. Where's the freedom in that?

Nell How d'you mean?

Mrs Marshall But now I'm none of those things, so what am I?

Doll Tastes of fucking horse piss.

Nell Don't drink it if you don't like it!

Mrs Marshall (*to Nell*) Now we've got the chance to be something different, new. Do you see?

Doll She ain't got no chances to be nothing.

Nell Stay out of it, Doll.

Doll No chances left. That's the point.

Nell (*to Mrs Marshall*) Don't take no notice of her.

Doll I got me faculties. I'm telling her.

Mrs Marshall Telling me?

Nell She's pissed.

Doll Someone has spoken out of turn. Said something. Betrayed you.

Mrs Marshall Betrayed me?

Doll He knows about the little wax man. The witchery.

Nell Who does?

Doll The Earl of Oxford.

Mrs Marshall Who said something?

Doll I never opened me mouth.

Nell What can he do? The Earl.

Doll They're still up to burning people.

Nell Burning them?

Doll Not a pleasant way to go.

Nell They wouldn't do that.

Mrs Marshall Wouldn't they? He hates me. (*Pause.*) I have to go. I can see that.

Nell We got shares now.

Doll Shares!

Mrs Marshall I'll have to live in some bloody cold place. Hidden. Quiet. Keeping my mouth shut.

Nell It won't come to that.

Mrs Marshall What will it come to? Just a flogging? That gets an audience. Would you stay for that?

Pause.

Nell Maybe you could start again, someplace.

Mrs Marshall Maybe. They found another word for me.

Doll Witch.

Mrs Marshall Before I could find one for myself. If they don't get you one way they get you another. (*She picks up the bag with Mrs Betterton's parts.*) Don't say I've been here.

Doll Leave your parts, then.

Mrs Marshall No. They're not having anything off me. (*Pause.*) He had a bad back and three teeth pulled. Also a lump on his neck. Fuck knows the state of his bollocks. Think of me.

Nell Good luck.

Mrs Marshall I'll burn these.

Doll Burn 'em?

Mrs Marshall indicates the parts and exits.

Nell I'd better get a move on. I'm late. Look out the window. See if there's a carriage.

Otway runs on clutching a script. He looks thin, untidy, ill.

Otway It's finished. It's finished. I wrote the last words last night and then I fell asleep hunched over the pages. So lucky. No more candles you see. Finished the last stump Friday. Then this morning woke up and read it through and it works! It really does. I think it really may be quite something. No longer than two and a half hours. Moving. I did cry. Amazing. There's this woman, Monimia, she's married but she takes a lover but she doesn't know she's taken a lover. I've called it *The Orphan*. I think it could be the making of me. I think Dad would be very proud.

Pause.

Nell Tell him, Doll.

Doll You're too late. She's scarpered. Goodbye.

Nell and Doll exit quickly.

Otway Too late? Story of my life. Story of my bloody life.

Throws his script down and wanders off.

Nell is on stage at the Duke's Playhouse, glowing.

Nell This is the epilogue and let me tell ye
    That none delivers it as good as Nellie.
    Tis my task to give the play summation
    It is indeed a test of concentration
    While some declare for that I am not fit
    Yet none can damn me for a lack of wit.
    If once I did serve gentlemen their waters
    Well now I am the envy of their daughters
    Yet some good citizens with apoplectic stutter
    Cry 'Be gad, sirs, the doxy's from the gutter'
    Well I say this, it's not stopped our duller poets
    (we know the agony they cause, we've all sat through it)
    From using Nell's finesse and matchless charms
    To add a little quality to their interminable yarns.
    So 'stead of the scurrilous sentiments to which you treat me
    Should be with heartfelt gratitude you greet me
    For, admit it, are you not the happier and hale
    To have this Nellie finish off our tale?

She curtsies and exits as if to great acclaim.

Nell is in her private tiring room at the Duke's.
Mrs Betterton and Doll enter.

Doll It's me an' her. We sneaked in round the back.

Nell Ain't you noticed? I'm on me own.

Doll Oh yeah.

Nell I have my own room. To myself.

Doll Innit lonely?

Nell No. It's private. Still, I've come a long way, ain't I? (*She picks up some parts.*) Look.

Doll What is it?

Nell It's a play.

Doll I'm sick of plays.

Nell It has a part for me. Especially written for me.

Doll What's someone want to write a part for you for?

Nell Because I'm a shining light upon our stage.

Doll And I'm the Queen of Sheba's uncle.

Nell That is what she said when she put the part into my hands.

Doll Who?

Nell Mrs Behn. She is the author.

Mrs Betterton A part written for Nell!

Doll (*to Nell*) You started her off now! (*to Mrs Betterton*) A lady did it.

Mrs Betterton Can they write plays?

Doll She has.

Mrs Betterton Is it performable?

Nell Don't be old fashioned.

Doll Mrs Betterton is old fashioned.

Mrs Betterton That is correct. You may blame longevity. You know, you have done quite well for yourself.

Nell Yes, I have.

Mrs Betterton Quite well indeed. I should like to think that I had a hand in it. A little hand in it. I would. I would. That is like a chink of light.

Doll That's nice. A chink of light.

Mrs Betterton Let us commence. Today's lesson. Affectation.

Doll (*to Nell*) Come on, come on, where's our shilling. We ain't doing it for nothing.

Nell All right. All right. It's in me purse. On the side.

Doll Mrs Betterton is vastly experienced and don't do lessons for sod all.

Nell I always pay, don't I?

Doll You are privileged to be in the presence of Mrs Betterton's presence.

Nell Am I? (*Pause.*) I don't want any more lessons.

Doll Yes you do.

Nell No. I don't.

Doll Yes, you do.

Mrs Betterton No. She does not.

Pause.

Nell He says he will buy me a house. A whole house. If I leave.

Mrs Betterton If you leave?

Nell It will have a large park attached. (*Pause.*) Plus a couple of peacocks, a footman, cutlery, plate, silver salvers, a necklace, half a hundred-weight of linen, best linen, and the loan of a horse and carriage.

Mrs Betterton That is a lot.

Doll That is a fucking fortune.

Mrs Betterton Yes, I can see that is a fucking fortune. It would be hard to turn down, I can see that.

Nell I'm not going because of what you think.

Doll Ain't you?

Nell No. I had a feeling.

Doll What you on about?

Nell I never had it before. In my gut. Like there was something there. Something curled up. Something ready to spread round my whole body. I never had it before. Not like that. A feeling.

Mrs Betterton Fear.

Nell Yes. That's what it was. Fear. I woke up and then suddenly I couldn't imagine what comes next. I tried to imagine but I couldn't. (*Pause.*) Nothing. If I stay here I'll just grow old and then what? (*Pause.*) A house with a park. Children.

Nell exits.

Doll Bloody hell.

Mrs Betterton gets up slowly.

You're not hearing them voices again?

Mrs Betterton begins to recite Lady Macbeth's final speech. She does it wonderfully in the grand old manner.

Mrs Betterton Yet here's a spot. Out, damned spot! Out, I
say! – One; two: Why, then 'tis time to do't. – Hell is
murky. – Fie, my Lord, fie! A soldier and afeard? – What
need we fear who knows it, when none can call our power
to account? – Yet who would have thought the old man to
have so much blood in him? The Thane of Fife had a wife:
where is she now? – What, will these hands ne'er be clean?
– No more o' that, my Lord, no more o' that; you mar all
with this starting. Here's the smell of the blood still; all the
perfumes of Arabia will not sweeten this little hand. Oh!
Oh! Oh! Wash your hands, put on your night-gown; look
not so pale. – I tell you again, Banquo's buried: he cannot
come out on's grave. To bed; to bed: there's knocking at
the gate. Come, come, come, come, give me your hand
what's done cannot be undone. To bed, to bed, to bed.
(*Pause.*) I know why she went mad, Doll. It was the
waiting, the waiting.

Doll You've not gone mad, have you?

Mrs Betterton Me? No. I'm just eccentric. Old and
eccentric. Come along.

She gets up slowly and exits.

Two years later, same room, Rochester on his death bed.
Mrs Barry in luxurious robe, counting money.

Doll Twenty-eight bags so far.

Mrs Barry Don't let them out of your sight, Doll.

Doll Sit on them, shall I?

Mrs Barry Yes, that would be best.

Doll (*indicating Rochester*) He's so quiet I keep thinking
he's a prop.

Mrs Barry Twenty-seven, twenty-eight . . .

Doll It don't seem right. You counting while he . . .

Mrs Barry (*louder*) Thirty shillings . . .

Doll One of his eyes is open. Look.

Rochester 'Nother drink.

Doll Shall I give him one . . .

Mrs Barry No. He hasn't got a liver.

Rochester Heartless whore. You're like a spider over that money. By rights half that's mine. All of it. I made you.

Mrs Barry Money won't help you where you're going. (*She continues to count.*)

Rochester I fell in love with you. That was my downfall. It made me turn to drink.

Mrs Barry You were drunk when we met.

Rochester I loved you.

Mrs Barry You made very interesting study. Unrequited love.

Rochester Money came between us.

Mrs Barry Luckily.

Rochester You loved me really. Please say it. (*His eyes close again.*)

Doll He's gone again. How long we've been awake?

Mrs Barry Two days.

Doll What we do?

Mrs Barry Keep counting. Two pounds, ten shillings and threepence halfpenny.

Doll Mrs B went very quick. She would have considered it impolite to hang about.

Mrs Barry Another bag.

Rochester wakes up.

Rochester I'm dying.

Mrs Barry One, two . . . and five is seven . . .

Rochester Say you loved me too. Say it. (*Pause.*) You know your problem. You haven't got any feelings. You've squeezed them out to make room for money and success. You think about it. When was the last time you really felt anything. I had too many feelings. That's why I had to drink. But I'd rather be dead dead than living dead like you. Oh you do a good imitation of feeling when you act, but it's an imitation. And soon when you stand up on a stage and try to imitate love or hate nothing will come out. Blank. You'll even have forgotten how the shadow of a feeling felt. You'll stand there squeaking. And the whole audience will know. They pick up things like that, like a beast scents blood, and they'll howl you off the stage. And then what'll happen? You'll sink, sink and my ghost will be there, laughing.

Mrs Barry You bastard. You helped me, I looked up to you. You were charismatic, I was grateful. I started to fall in love. But then I thought I know what will happen. You'll tire. I'd be miserable then I'd be cast off, a pauper. There seemed no way out. But luckily I turned out to be an extremely talented actress. Beyond my wildest dreams. I had all the love I wanted – on stage. And then later I went home, safe, and counted my money. You just can't bear it because I've won.

Doll He's dead, love.

Mrs Barry Dead? (*Pause.*) Cover him over, Doll.

A woman appears in the doorway.

Doll Visitor, ma'am.

Mrs Barry Thank you, Doll. (*She looks up.*) Yes?

Nell Favour.

Mrs Barry I'm not a charity.

Nell Not money.

Mrs Barry What then?

Nell Look. Used to be my room.

Mrs Barry Yours?

Doll Bloody heck.

Mrs Barry Language.

Doll It's Mrs Gwyn.

Mrs Barry Mrs Gwyn?

Nell Just wanted a look.

Mrs Barry Of course. Of course. Show her my costume, Doll.

Doll does so.

Doll Monimia.

Nell Very nice. (*She hugs the dress.*)

Doll Come on. (*Doll tries to take it away.*)

Mrs Barry Let her hold it, Doll.

Nell still hugs the dress.

Doll What's happened to you?

Nell Sick.

Doll Poxed. Just like the King. God rest his soul.

Mrs Barry I don't feel anything.

Doll Well it's a year ago now.

Mrs Barry About him. Rochester.

Nell is rocking herself with the dress. Doll tries to tell a story to calm them down, slowly they begin to listen to her.

Doll Before this place turned playhouse it was a bear pit. My dad was the bear keeper. One day this bear turned on him. The whip came down and down on her but still she came. Slashed his chest here to here. That night they took out her claws and teeth. Ripped them out. And she howled and screamed and rocked in pain. There was blood on the floor. 'No, Dad, no,' I says. And he said, 'You let one of them get away with it and tomorrow none of them bears'll dance.' The bear had gone still and her head was hanging and I said 'Why should you whip her?' He took my hand and put it in the blood that was on the floor and then he wiped more on my face. 'She dances and we eat meat,' he said. 'Never let me hear you speak on it again.' The blood was warm at first and then it started turning cold on me and it seemed to turn me cold. I never did say nothing again.

Pause. Both Nell and Mrs Barry are looking at her.

Till now. Playhouse creatures they called you like you was animals. What I always thought but never said out aloud till now was I was glad she went for him. I was glad she did it. She had spirit.

Mrs Barry (*completely calm*) Yes, yes, she did. (*She continues to count her money.*)

Nell begins to dance with the dress.

Nell Beautiful.

THE POSITIVE HOUR

Characters

Nicola
Paula
Miranda
Emma
The Man
Roger
Victoria

The Positive Hour was first performed at Hampstead
Theatre, London, on 27 February 1997 with the
following cast:

Nicola Kate Ashfield
Paula Julia Lane
Miranda Margot Leicester
Emma Patti Love
The Man David Sibley
Roger Robin Soans
Victoria Holly Searson or Kitty Stafford-Clark

Directed by Max Stafford-Clark
Designed by Julian McGowan
Lighting by Johanna Town
Sound by Scott Myers

Act One

SCENE ONE

Miranda's office. Miranda sits at her desk. Paula enters.

Paula I don't want any more bollocks.

Miranda Pardon?

Paula Bollocks.

Miranda Now, Paula . . .

Paula I'm a desperate woman. You must've seen one of us before? We smoke and have hastily applied mascara. It's my daughter. Victoria Savage. Eight and three-quarters. Her favourite groups are Spice Girls and Michael Jackson. I haven't got the heart to tell her he's a pervert. I mean, children are in their own special world, aren't they?

Miranda I've got your file here.

Paula Temporarily fostered with the Clements. Mr and Mrs Patrick of Sussex. They don't like me going there. They say it upsets Victoria. Course it does. I'm her mother. It's a wrench when I leave. She cries, I cry. It's a fucking mess. Patrick's a bank manager and Isobel doesn't know what to do with herself. They have a mug tree. Know the sort? Victoria's a very demanding child. That house was dead and now they're wetting themselves with having a bit of life in their life, but it's my fucking bit of life.

Miranda Paula, fostering is a temporary arrangement and every effort is made to return the child to its mother.

Paula So they say.

Miranda This is my first morning, Paula. You probably

know that I've been away for a bit. I just wanted the opportunity to meet you and to discuss your situation.

Paula You see, this thing has happened in their heads. Somehow they think they are Victoria's parents and I am a passing annoyance.

Miranda I'm sure that's not the case.

Paula And people are going to look at them and look at me and think she's better off with them. But she's my daughter.

Miranda A child is always better off with its mother unless there are serious concerns for its welfare.

Paula Do you like me?

Miranda I haven't introduced myself. Miranda Hurst.

Paula Because it's important, isn't it, Miranda, that you like me? What you think is important?

Miranda My assessment will have a bearing on the outcome of your case, but it would be bad practice if I let personal opinion interfere with professional judgement.

Paula So what are you going to do about Victoria?

Miranda Well, there's nothing I can do today.

Paula No one's listening to me.

Miranda Of course we want to place your daughter back with you. That's terribly important, but what we have to do is to see that as a goal at the end of a longer term process.

Paula A process?

Miranda Yes.

Paula Five months now they've had her.

Miranda Yes, Paula.

Paula So how long's a process?

Miranda It's as long as it takes.

Paula I'm sick of people keep putting me off.

Miranda Paula . . .

Paula Don't fucking Paula me. (*She pulls a razor blade out of her bag and holds it to her wrist.*) Don't even fucking move.

Miranda Please, Paula, put that away.

Paula I'm never happy, not without Victoria. I wake up in the morning and it's like there's a big hole in my chest only I'm too scared to look down because once I do I'm going to feel this pain.

Miranda It must be very hard. Now, please, let's be calm.

Paula No. Let's be hysterical. Let's have blood.

Miranda Of course we must start the whole thing moving now.

Paula Moving, that's good, Miranda.

Miranda Because, believe me, I want your daughter to be given back to you very much. The problems are solvable. I will have failed if we don't get Victoria back with you and I don't want to fail. Why don't you sit down and put that away and then we can begin.

Pause. Paula sits down and places the blade near to her on the desk between them.

Paula I'm putting it here.

Miranda Actually I had a sort of collapse. An exhaustion thing. After six months my doctor said, 'Yes, go back to work, but avoid stressful situations.' This is my first day.

Paula Oh. Sorry.

Miranda opens Paula's file.

Miranda We think it was a virus.

Paula There's a lot of weird things about.

Miranda Well. I'd just like to go over a few details to start with. Accommodation, has anything changed?

Paula No.

Miranda You're still in a bedsit?

Paula I'm on the council waiting-list. Lewisham.

Miranda I'll try giving them a ring. See if we can get any movement on that. You're claiming job-seekers' allowance?

Paula Yes.

Miranda Are you looking for work?

Paula No.

Miranda I think it's important not to become defeated.

Paula looks blank.

Work is a stabilizer. It's also one way out of bedsit land. That would be a plus for Victoria living with you again. Having a criminal record doesn't mean that you're unemployable.

Paula Doesn't help though, does it, Miranda? Do one stupid thing and it follows you for life. I stole a poxy video cassette recorder. Three months in Holloway. That's how I lost Victoria.

Miranda And Michael?

Paula Michael?

Miranda Victoria told the Clements that she was scared of Michael.

Paula That must be from when I broke my arm. I told them it was an accident.

Miranda How did that happen?

Paula I broke it and she thought he broke it but she was mixed up. Kids do get mixed up. Have you got kids?

Miranda No. Victoria says he broke it and she's frightened he'll break her arm.

Paula It was an accident.

Miranda How often does he hit you?

Paula The arm was a one-off thing. He's never hit her.

Miranda She just has to watch him hitting you. Does he live with you?

Paula On and off.

Miranda It doesn't sound like a very sustaining relationship.

Paula He's my boyfriend. I'm not like a punch bag. It's not like that. Just when we have fights.

Miranda There's never an excuse for a man to hit a woman.

Paula The longer they have Victoria the less likely it is I'll get her back.

Miranda That's not true.

Paula Fuck off, it is. She's my daughter. Sometimes I wake up and I lie there and I can't get up. I can't think of a reason to get up.

Miranda But at the same time there are positive steps you can take, Paula. You could decide to leave a violent man. Do things that are in your power first.

Paula I love him though.

Miranda It's a question of priorities, isn't it?

Paula It would help, if I got rid of him.

Miranda Absolutely. Anything that demonstrates your desire to provide a good home for your daughter. And wouldn't it be a positive step for you?

Paula Do you think I'll be able to leave him?

Miranda Yes. I do. I've often found people have a great deal more in them than they realize.

SCENE TWO

Emma in a stranger's flat. She looks about her.

Emma How long have you been in banking? (*Pause.*) I think it's fascinating what you were saying about index linking. (*Pause.*) I feel a bit light-headed actually. I shouldn't drink on an empty stomach but I always do. It's stupid because the next morning you pay for it. (*Pause.*) This is the sort of thing you're always told not to do. Going back to a stranger's house. But then how do you get to know someone if you don't see their home? You get to know them a lot quicker than if you were just sitting in a pub. You've got pictures on the wall. I like pictures. (*She looks at them.*) Is that a Tillier? He's marvellous, isn't he? With him a smudge isn't a smudge, is it? It's movement. So have you ever used one of these agencies before? (*Pause.*) I used to think it was a degrading idea. An agency. That only social misfits used them. Which of

course is totally untrue. I mean, look at us. (*Pause.*) What
are you up to in there?

*The door opens and a man enters. He is naked from the
waist up and he wears a black hood, studded collar and
belt.*

Oh my God. (*Pause.*) I think you've got the wrong idea
about me. Absolutely and utterly the wrong idea. I have
to go now. (*She grabs her stuff.*) I'm not like that. I just
wanted to talk.

Hooded Man OK.

He sits down. Emma heads to the door. Stops.

Emma I really am not into that. I'm a feminist and a
pacifist. I've never hurt anyone in my life.

Hooded Man Of course.

Emma You seemed nice. But that's the thing with men –
you can never tell. It's the same as with my ex-husband.
One day he just turned round and said, 'We've grown
apart.' Just like that.

Hooded Man Very upsetting.

Emma Devastating.

Hooded Man Absolutely.

Pause.

Emma I can hear a dog barking somewhere. I thought
about getting a dog when Alan left but then I couldn't
bear the idea of all that hair on the cushions. Pit-bulls are
becoming very common. Three kids and a pit-bull. In
working-class families. You know, the revolutionary
masses. Alan was a Trotskyist for years but then it sort of
wore off. About the time the housing market went
through the roof. Now he's got a restaurant. For the last

three years of our marriage he didn't want sex, he just wanted to do the menus.

Hooded Man You talk a lot.

Emma Is there anything wrong with that?

Hooded Man No. It was a comment. Hit me.

Emma What?

Hooded Man gives her a long black glove.

Hooded Man On the legs. With that.

Emma This is absolutely ridiculous.

Hooded Man Go on.

Pause. Emma takes the glove and hits him.

Hooded Man Thank you.

Emma This really isn't me. (*She makes to exit.*)

Hooded Man Don't go.

Emma I'm sorry. I'm normal. (*She exits quickly.*)

SCENE THREE

Paula and Miranda. Miranda's office.

Paula Well, I did it. This is how I did it. I drank neat vodka. Then I taped a note to my door which said, 'It's over, love Paula.' Then I left his reproduction Armani underpants in a plastic bag on the mat. Then I hid. Mastermind. Only I never closed my window. 2 a.m., I wake up and he's looming over me. 'Fuck you, Paula,' he said. 'Fuck you, Michael,' I said. That went on for a bit. I said, 'I'm sorry, Michael, but what can I do? I have to demonstrate my desire to provide a good home for my

daughter.' He tried snogging. It didn't work. Well, it did
for about two minutes. But, anyway. Cut to me an hour
later. More vodka had been swilled. More tears had
watered the ashtray. I was doing it. I didn't even know
why I was doing it. Finally, I took the taped note off the
door and stuck it on my forehead. I said, 'Michael, it's not
that I don't think you're a decent bloke underneath, but
who's got a spade big enough to shovel off all the shit?'
(*She turns slightly to one side.*) That's how I got my eye.
This morning I woke up and I swear I felt like Bambi. I
lay there for a bit just listening to the sounds coming in
the window and I thought, this is nice.

Miranda I think that was a very sensible move to make.

Paula Sensible? How about fucking huge?

Miranda Well, let's just see how things go.

Paula How do you mean?

Miranda Over the next month or so.

Paula The next month?

Miranda See how things pan out.

Paula Another month?

Miranda That's only reasonable. Don't you think?

Paula What about the rest of it? My flat?

Miranda I'm waiting for Lewisham housing to phone me
back.

Paula Don't hold your breath. I have to have something,
Miranda. I can't stay in that room with less than I had
before. Do you know?

Miranda Have you thought any more about work?

Paula No.

Miranda There's a sense of self to be found in work, Paula. It can mean more than just economic independence. I don't want to force anything on you. What I'd like ideally is for us to be in a kind of partnership. Working on your situation together. Both contributing.

Paula I just want Victoria back.

Miranda I can't just give her back to you. You know that. (*Pause.*) I think this is an opportunity for you, Paula. To do more than just get back what you've lost. To imagine better for yourself and go for it. Perhaps the issue here is retraining of some sort. I have a client who is taking a GCSE.

Paula A what?

Miranda A GCSE. In ancient history. The Romans fascinated her. Apparently they had central-heating systems.

Paula Lucky bastards. What does she want to be, a central-heating engineer?

Miranda No.

Paula A centurion?

Miranda I should think that would be difficult. Was there a subject that particularly interested you at school?

Paula No.

Miranda Well, how do you see your future?

Paula I could meet a rich man. I could win the lottery.

Miranda That's a bit of a gamble.

Paula It's better than nothing.

Miranda I think it is pretty much nothing, don't you? The job centre could give you retraining information. We could discuss it together. Will you think about it?

Paula All right.

Miranda I think you could build a real future for your-self, Paula. Don't you?

Paula Miranda, can I ask you a favour? I'm visiting Victoria at the weekend. I haven't got the train fare. Twenty quid. Is there any chance of me borrowing it?

Miranda Yes, all right. (*Gives Paula money.*)

Paula Thanks, partner. (*She begins to go.*)

Miranda I'm starting a small group, Paula. Just a few of us. We'd meet regularly. Starting Tuesday. A sort of sup-port group. We'd share advice. Discuss our feelings.

Paula What for?

Miranda I think it's a creative way to work. Are you interested?

Paula No thanks. That sort of thing makes me feel nau-seous. (*She goes to exit again.*)

Miranda It would look like you're making an effort, wouldn't it? Taking some control. You might even enjoy it.

Paula hesitates momentarily before she exits. Miranda, who has taken her coat, hurries out.

SCENE FOUR

The group meets. A semi-circle of chairs. Nicola sits hold-ing her bag. Paula enters.

Paula Is this the group?

Nicola What?

Paula The group?

Nicola Oh, the group. Yes, yes, it is.

Paula Right. You're not exactly what I'd have called a group.

Nicola My name's Nicola.

Paula Paula.

Nicola You can call me Nick or Nicky. Or Nicola.

Paula Right.

Pause.

Nicola Soon we won't be nervous. After a couple of meetings our nerves will wear off. Then we won't be able to remember what it was like to feel . . . nervous.

Paula What's in that bag, Nicky?

Nicola My bag?

Paula 'Cos if it's alive you'll have squeezed all the juices out of it by now.

Nicola It's just books. I take them out with me because I don't like leaving them at home.

Paula Why's that?

Nicola It's just a feeling.

Paula It's lucky you don't feel that way about the chairs.

Nicola Oh, no. That would be mad.

Paula Yes. What sort of group is this, anyway?

Nicola A woman's group.

Paula Fuck. Is it?

Nicola Miranda must have mentioned it.

Paula I must have suppressed it. Are you a client of Miranda's?

Nicola Off and on. We keep in touch. We thought it might be a good idea if I came along. I think it's a positive thing for women to meet in this way. To share and empower. I was in two groups before. (*Pause.*) After a bit it begins to work. It's wonderful the way it works. We tell each other things you never imagine you will. (*Pause.*) The reason I didn't leave my books at home is because once I came back and they were in the bath. Floating in the bath. My dad. Afterwards he's sorry.

Paula I think groups are crap. My presence here is tactical.

Emma enters. Flustered.

Emma I'm looking for Miranda.

Paula She's not here.

Emma She should be here.

Paula But she's not here.

Nicola She'll be here in a minute. Have you come for the group?

Emma Well, now I don't know what to do. I probably haven't brought a pen. (*She rummages in her bag.*)

Paula What are you in for?

Emma What? Oh. I'm not . . . I'm a friend of Miranda's. I'm not . . . shit. I'll leave her a note. (*She roots in her bag once more.*) No pen. Could you say that Emma came. She came and she had to go. Something came up. Thank you for suggesting I came in the first place. I'm all right. I just have to pull myself together. Love Emma. So. Emma. Came. Went. OK now. Sorry. Love etc. . . .

Miranda enters and Emma sits down quickly.

Shit.

Miranda Hello. Have you all met?

They nod. Miranda sits.

I'll just say a few words as it's our first meeting. Welcome. I know it isn't easy joining a group and I want to say congratulations for getting here. For taking that first step. In the past I've found that groups such as these can offer the support and encouragement necessary to enable us to create positive change in our lives at stressful or difficult times. I've kept it women only because, well, it speaks for itself really. (*Pause.*) Women often find it easier to share in an all-woman environment. (*Pause.*) Would anyone like to start?

Pause. They sit in silence.

Nicola I'd just like to say that I'm very glad to be here.

Emma I don't think I should be here. I'm sorry, Miranda. I was just feeling confused. I must be at a sort of turning point in my life. But turning to what? Miranda . . . we're friends . . . is it OK to tell them, Miranda? I'm not really one of you. Miranda was telling me about the group and then I just thought, God, I'm in such a mess. I have to do something. This is my opportunity. This group. But now, sitting here, I'm thinking what on earth was I thinking?

Miranda People often feel uncomfortable at the first meeting.

Nicola I could start if you like?

Miranda That's very generous of you, Nicola. Nicola was in a group I ran before.

Nicola My dad doesn't like me going out of the flat. I

hink he's scared of being on his own. I'm finding it quite
ard to leave him on his own.

Miranda I think we should start with some role work.
You be yourself, Nicola.

Nicola stands.

Emma, would you be Nicola's dad?

Nicola Geoff.

Emma Geoff?

Miranda Emma, you respond to Nicola as if you were
Geoff.

Emma But what sort of person is he?

Miranda A person that doesn't like being alone.

Emma That could be anybody.

Paula A desperate fucker.

Miranda We used this technique before very successfully,
didn't we, Nicola?

Nicola Yes.

Emma But what do I say?

Nicola Dad?

Emma Have we started?

Nicola Dad?

Emma Yes? I'm sorry I've forgotten your name.

Nicola Nicola. I'm going out now, Dad.

Emma Out?

Nicola Yes. Out.

Emma Out?

Nicola Yes.

Emma OK, Nicola.

Nicola Don't get upset, Dad.

Emma I'm not getting upset.

Nicola Well, you usually do. You usually tell me not to go.

Emma Oh. Don't go.

Nicola I have to, Dad. I'm studying. My exams are next month.

Emma Well, all right then. Seeing as it's your education that's at stake.

They stop there. Nicola looks over to Miranda.

Miranda I think you got your permission to leave a little easily, Nicola. But you remained calm and logical, which was an effective strategy. Do you want to say anything?

Nicola I thought Emma did very well.

Emma I was awful.

Miranda Try swapping over.

Nicola You can have my bag. He sits in the chair facing the telly.

She gives her bag to Emma. Sits down, centre.

Miranda (*to Emma*) You're Nicola.

Emma Oh. I see. I'm Nicola. (*She prepares herself and begins.*) I'm going out now, Dad. I have my exams to do. I want to get on in life. So I'm going out now. Goodbye.

Nicola stares straight ahead.

I said goodbye. (*Pause.*) Aren't you going to say goodbye back?

Nicola Drip drip drip.

Emma What?

Nicola There's a drip, Nick. Kitchen ceiling.

Emma I'll have a look when I get back.

Nicola Are you going to pass then?

Emma That's the idea.

Nicola Then off to college. Wizz bang. Corks pop. A degree used to be a passport to something. To a job actually. That was in the old days when there were jobs. Seriously though, Nick, a vocational degree is better than some piss-farty thing. Psychology.

Emma Well, I have to be going.

Nicola Psych-ology. What am I going to do?

Emma You can watch the telly.

Nicola Five o'clock, Nick.

Emma Another hour and it'll get going.

Nicola Excessive use of hyperbole, Nick. Telly never gets going. Telly is a stream of pale lumpless puke that consistently fails to become projectile.

Emma Oh, well. Read the paper.

Nicola Have you read it?

Emma No.

Nicola Too much time on my hands, that's my problem. I've read it. What's your opinion on wine, Nick?

Emma It's a drink.

Nicola Education's not been wasted on you, has it? There's one whole page given over to the glory of wine. A picture too, just in case we don't know what a bottle looks like. Pinot Noir, Pouilly Fuisse. I don't expect it means anything to you, does it? Could be dog's-piss wine, couldn't it? French – much too sensible a subject. No 'ology' in it.

Emma I don't drink wine.

Nicola You need money to drink it. Is that what you mean? And I could never afford it?

Emma No.

Nicola I'm thinking of the future. I worry about you, Nick. There you'll be one day, discussing psychology and drinking arse water. We are the hollow men. I've upset myself now. Skip your class. Just this once, Nick. I feel low.

Emma I can't.

Nicola It can't hurt, can it? Just to miss it once. I don't want to be on my own, Nick. Not tonight. I get these thoughts.

Emma Well, you could save them up and tell them to me later. When I get back. After I've been out.

Nicola Aren't you handling me well? Wouldn't your friend Miranda be pleased. You've contained my aggressive negativity. Skip it. This once. Won't hurt. For me. Please. Please, love. Please.

Emma seems stuck.

We could talk.

Emma is still stuck. Nicola comes to her rescue.

But you've made a commitment.

Emma Yes.

Nicola That's right. To yourself.

Emma Yes.

Nicola Bye, love.

Emma manages to leave.

Miranda Well done, Nicola and Emma.

Emma How incredible. I mean, it was actually quite difficult to get out of the door.

Miranda Yes, he was making it hard for you.

Nicola He does love me. He's not like that all the time.

Emma He just kept talking. It's hard to say what about.

Miranda But you kept hold of your initial desire to leave.

Nicola He doesn't really talk to anyone except me.

Emma That was very interesting.

Miranda He uses that. You have rights too.

Emma I knew I was right to come. It's great to be here. Inspiring. Like old times.

Miranda Is there anything you'd like to say, Paula?

Paula Do we get a tea break?

SCENE FIVE

Miranda at home. She is working. Roger comes in from the kitchen. He has a bottle of wine and glasses.

Roger You're not working?

Miranda Yes, Roger, I am. I'm behind. Terribly behind.

Roger But you've only been back a fortnight. Friday night. Shouldn't you be taking things easy? Slowly but surely.

Miranda There is no such animal in social work.

Roger They did say, didn't they, at work, that you should take it easy? I was there, remember. The afternoon you came home.

Miranda I'm absolutely fine.

Roger Yes, of course. Of course you are.

Miranda Working helps.

Roger I've got some wine. I thought we could have a toast. To the old Miranda. It's good to have her back.

Miranda I'll have one later, thanks.

Roger Right, right.

Miranda I really do just have to finish this. (*She continues to work.*)

Roger I suppose I could do some work. (*He doesn't move.*) Yes. I don't seem to get time for it nowadays. You know, four years ago no one in my department had even heard the word module. Now everything's modules, modules. The whole department has gone modular. It's like a disease. A module is like a pill, you hand it to your students with a glass of water and say, 'Here, swallow when you can afford it.' (*He pours himself a drink.*) I looked it up the other day. A set course forming a unit in an educational scheme. Little words. Scheme: a plan pursued secretly, insidiously for private ends. Yes, I thought. Yes. Where have all the big words gone? Enlightenment. Growth.

Miranda Roger.

Roger Sorry. Sorry. (*Pause.*) The thing is, I spend half my

ime administrating my modules. They come with twice
heir bodyweight in paper. Where am I supposed to get
any time for my bloody Hegel?

Miranda It is harder now, Roger, but you'll make time.

Roger Yes, yes. You need a good text behind you in order
o create the right sort of modular appeal.

Miranda (*still working*) You've got a text behind you.

Roger Fifteen years behind me. It doesn't count.

Miranda You could do some work now.

Roger ponders this. Sound of someone entering.

Roger That's Emma. I think the idea is we have a bit of a
celebration.

Miranda I'm working.

He jumps up. Emma enters, carrying a bag of shopping.

Emma Happy second week back!

Miranda Thank you.

Emma I went along to Miranda's group, Roger. It was
fantastic. I'm cooking. (*She indicates the bag.*) Shall we
have a drink? Oh, Roger's started! Yes please, Roger.

*Roger pours her a drink. Miranda puts her work to one
side.*

I'd just like to say a few things. About me. You've been
brilliant, both of you. Such good friends. Letting me treat
this like a second home, listening to me go on and on about
Alan. It must have been really boring. Anyway, cheers.

Roger It wasn't boring. Was it, Miranda?

Miranda It's fantastic that you're on your feet again,
Emma.

Emma Yes. In fact I just wanted to run something by you.

Roger Sure.

Emma The thing is, I don't want criticism. I feel that what I need at this point are warm agreeing eyes looking at me.

Roger OK.

Miranda How can we approve of something before we've heard what it is?

Emma I knew you'd be critical.

Miranda Well, I could leave the room for five minutes and Roger can sit here nodding and smiling. How's that?

Emma That would be silly. It's your house. Well, just let me finish what I have to say before you interrupt. (*Pause.*) I met this woman. She has a business in occasion cards and she wants to expand and she's looking for a partner. Someone with a good eye. Artistic flair. I could put in some of the money that Alan gave me. New occasions are being invented all the time. Congratulations on your first holiday together card. Or, sorry to hear of the death of your pet.

Pause.

Miranda What about your painting?

Emma I knew you'd say that. I haven't done that for a while, Miranda. That's what I've been trying to tell you.

Miranda But you'll start again soon.

Emma I just don't seem to get round to it.

Miranda It's Alan's fault. He used you, Emma.

Emma Yes, I know.

Miranda Chopping his salads when you should have been doing your work.

Emma I know. I was stupid. But sometimes he couldn't get the staff.

Miranda He couldn't get them for free.

Emma Alan was paying the mortgage. I felt guilty.

Miranda Well, it's over now. You can get back to what you want to do.

Emma These cards.

Miranda You can't be serious about this, Emma. You're an artist. You don't want to get involved in some half-baked business venture that'll collapse in six months.

Emma She seemed a nice woman.

Pause.

Miranda Do you know where I drove past yesterday? Salt Street.

Roger Did you?

Miranda It's been converted into flats. We could never afford a house like that now. I stopped the car and looked. It always seemed such a sunny house.

Emma That's to do with the position of the windows.

Miranda And memories. Good memories.

Emma If Alan was here it could be like then – the four of us.

Miranda But Alan isn't here.

Emma No. Alan is officially a bastard. (*Pause.*) What I remember is talking. Lots of people talking and talking. You and Roger stayed up for nights discussing whether his penis was an instrument of patriarchy.

Roger It rings a faint bell.

Miranda We found a *Playboy* in Alan's room and we ritually burnt it, didn't we, Emma?

Emma You'd read *The Female Eunuch*.

Miranda I remember feeling fantastic. Watching it burn.

Roger Arguably the most radical revolution of the twentieth century is the feminist one. Woman shaking off her chains.

Miranda And your painting is part of that, Emma.

Emma Roger's got a little paunch!

Roger Oh God, have I?

Emma Just then you looked like a faun, Roger. A saggy old faun.

Roger God, how alarming.

Emma Yes, we're all getting older.

Miranda What a revelation.

Roger The thing is, I'm not sure what position I take on jogging.

Emma What position?

Roger Politically. For me jogging has become the primary spectacle of the mass leisure market. The nexus of sport and capitalism.

Miranda Also you've lost one of your trainers.

Emma Alan goes jogging. He's very up on these things. He's in a men's group now, Roger.

Roger Jesus, is he?

Miranda That's no bad thing.

Roger I suppose not.

Miranda Men wanting to empower women.

Emma It's not that sort of group, Miranda. This is a nineties version. They go into the woods and beat drums. It helps them succeed in business. It's an American import. It's very primeval and that's why they're always jogging.

Roger Extraordinary.

Miranda Pathetic.

Emma With jogging you have to have a planned programme, Roger. London's full of poor old joggers dropping dead from sudden exertion.

Miranda Roger's not old, he's fifty-one.

Roger Fifty. Fifty!

Miranda Fifty-one.

Roger Jesus. Am I?

Emma Marlon Brando.

Roger That's incredible.

Emma He's fat but he still gets fucked.

Roger Somehow psychologically I'd lost a year.

Emma So you see you've no need to worry, Roger.

Miranda You're obsessed.

Emma Obsessed?

Miranda With bodies, age.

Emma It's all right for you. You've got Roger.

Miranda I haven't 'got' anybody.

Emma You're not trawling like I am.

Miranda Trawling?

Emma Picking over the scrawny left-behinds for life's partner. It's so degrading. I could kill Alan. He only had to stick around another twenty years and then he would have died. I don't want to be alone for the rest of my life.

Miranda You don't have to be alone.

Emma I'm forty-six. I have no significant other.

Miranda You have friends, Emma. You have your work.

Emma But who'll go on holiday with me? Who do I plan my retirement home with? I don't know if I can hold down another meal for one!

Miranda You're making yourself sound desperate.

Emma I'm sorry. That's how I feel. (*Pause.*) Are you where you expected to be, Miranda?

Miranda Approximately.

Emma Do you wish you'd ever had children?

Miranda No.

Emma Somehow you seem to be on track and I don't seem to be.

Miranda You're just healing. Getting over something.

Emma When Alan left I got down on my hands and knees and begged him to stay.

Miranda Oh.

Emma If you think about it, 'Oh' is just a hole.

Miranda It's an expression of mild concern.

Emma It's a hole. What do holes stand for? Graves or emptiness. Alan was my bung. The bung to stuff up my hole. My problem is I've lost my bung.

Roger I'm beginning to feel a twinge on Alan's behalf.

Emma I sleep with his coat. I try to be strong and worthy of your friendship but I just don't seem able to manage it.

Miranda Things will get better, Emma.

Emma What if they don't?

Miranda Well, I suppose that's up to you. You can decide you can't survive in the big wicked world without Alan. Or you can face things and be a human being. You've got us. We'll support you.

Emma You're right. Of course you're right. You've been very good to me. I'll start the food. (*She exits quickly.*)

Roger Do you want some help?

A smashing sound. Emma re-enters holding broken bowl.

Emma I'm sorry.

Miranda Don't worry.

Emma Oh. God, I'm so clumsy.

Miranda It's only a bowl. Don't worry.

Emma But it was your favourite. I must be feeling a bit shaky. I'm sorry.

Roger We'll be able to glue that.

Emma God, I'm useless sometimes. And I've forgotten the cream. I'll go round the corner.

Roger I'll go, shall I?

Emma No, no. My mistake. (*She takes her coat, hurries out.*)

Miranda Might as well throw that away. (*Indicates bowl.*)

Roger Really?

Miranda It's a sort of aggression against me. I don't want to be reminded of it.

Roger Against you?

Miranda Lost people hate us because they need us.

Roger Is Emma lost?

Miranda What do you think?

Roger But Emma never used to be lost. How would someone know if they were lost?

Miranda You're not lost, Roger.

Roger Oh, I know that. I know that. I was just thinking,

Miranda My clients make our lives look like heaven.

Roger Sure, sure. We're steeped in privilege. (*Pause.*) Have a drink?

Miranda You have a drink. I must get on.

Roger I just thought we could have a drink together.

SCENE SIX

The intercom. We hear Emma's voice in the dark: 'Hello.' The buzz of the intercom. The Hooded Man lets Emma into his flat.

Emma Do you always wear that?

Hooded Man When I knew it was you. In your honour.

Emma You needn't have bothered. I'm bringing these back. (*She shows him the gloves.*)

Hooded Man Oh.

Emma I left with them last time. It was a mistake.

Hooded Man Thanks.

Emma I wasn't sure you'd be in. I was going to push them through the letter box. I'm actually a very honest person.

Hooded Man Yes. Thank you. Would you like a drink?

Emma No. I better go.

Hooded Man Well. Thanks. (*He holds up the gloves.*)

Emma You should have said something.

Hooded Man I should have. You're right.

Emma You shouldn't have just sprung it on me. Coming out of the bathroom like that.

Hooded Man I know. I apologize.

Emma It's not what you expect on a first date.

Hooded Man Sorry. To be honest, I thought it might be best to plunge you straight in.

Emma Plunge me?

Hooded Man Rubberists are experiencing a scarcity of female partners.

Emma You do surprise me.

Hooded Man But with you I took a gamble.

Emma Why?

Hooded Man I don't know. I was acting on instinct I suppose.

Emma Do you mean that you instinctively saw something in me?

Hooded Man Just an instinct.

Emma What did you see?

Hooded Man And then I knew when you took the gloves.

Emma Knew what?

Hooded Man I suppose it's a primitive thing. An exchange.

Emma I felt awkward, that's why I took them. I felt socially compromised.

Hooded Man Accepting something. It's a pun.

Emma Don't go all bloody literary on me.

Hooded Man You have a natural proclivity to anger. I like that.

Emma I'm not an angry person.

Hooded Man I think people get strait-jacketed into what's considered a normal sex life and then they never feel free to experiment. Then they have to be shocked into something new.

Emma Plunged.

Hooded Man Yes.

Emma How did you get into all this rubber?

Hooded Man With a wellington boot. As a child I was repeatedly struck on the buttocks with a wellington boot.

Emma Really?

Hooded Man No. Not at all. I just like rubber. It's slippery, smooth and it twangs.

Emma I think you must have some sort of dreadful problem.

Hooded Man I just like to unwind in my free time.

Emma Why don't you play golf like other people?

Hooded Man You were getting into it.

Emma I was not.

Hooded Man It seemed to me that you were getting into it.

Emma It's just silly. Inside I was laughing at how stupid you looked.

Hooded Man There was a connection between us in the eyes.

Emma I was thinking, God, this is one for the diary.

Hooded Man It's not the sort of game you can play on your own. That's how I know. From when you took the gloves.

Emma Bollocks to the gloves. You see, this is all so typically male. Violence is sexy. And there's no feelings. Nothing between us. It's all to do with patriarchy. I even bother to return your poxy property. A typical caring woman. Really I should burn the f-ing things.

Hooded Man You are a goddess.

Emma My name is Emma.

Hooded Man Please burn them. They cost twenty four pounds.

Emma You evil little worm.

Hooded Man gets to his knees.

Hooded Man I'm wriggling at your feet.

Emma You ought to be careful. I could be insane. I must be when you stop to think about it. I could put my foot on your neck and crush it and crush it till it snapped.

Hooded Man Put your foot on my neck.

Emma You really are asking for trouble.

Hooded Man I know.

Emma I could do it.

Hooded Man I know.

Emma I could. (*Pause.*) Oh God. Oh my God.

Hooded Man What?

Emma Something terrible has happened.

Hooded Man What?

Emma I want to press harder.

Hooded Man Press harder.

Emma I want to press harder.

Hooded Man We can swap over later. I've got a spare hood in the bedroom.

He exits, she follows.

SCENE SEVEN

Paula in Miranda's office. 7 p.m. She has Victoria on her lap. Victoria is eating a packet of crisps.

Paula Don't tell me. I know. I know. I did a stupid thing. I couldn't help myself. We just got on the train, didn't we, Victoria?

Victoria eats, nods.

We had a brilliant day. We went to *Baywatch the Movie*. Then we went to Burger King. I said to Victoria, do you want to go back to the Clements or do you want to come home with me, and she said, I want to come home with you, Mum, didn't you?

Victoria We had king-size chips.

Miranda I'll phone the Clements now. (*She picks up phone, dials.*)

Paula I know it looks bad.

Victoria When that man was drowning, right, how come he wasn't eaten by a shark?

Paula Because it wasn't a film with a shark in. Sharks cost money. It was a cheap film.

Miranda Hello. Hello. It's Miranda Hurst. Yes. Yes. She's here with me now.

Paula Don't stuff all those in at once, Victoria. It's not nice.

Victoria I'm chewing them.

Paula You're swallowing them whole.

Miranda Well, if that's convenient for you.

Victoria chews open-mouthed to demonstrate.

Victoria We're doing Africa at school, Mum.

Paula Yeah.

Miranda Yes, of course.

Victoria Africa's a continent not a country.

Paula Shhh. No one said it was a country.

Miranda That would be fine.

Victoria It's a very common mistake to make.

Paula What's that on your T-shirt?

Victoria It's called Eurocentrism.

Paula It's called ice-cream.

Miranda Thank you so much.

She tickles Victoria, who laughs.

Mr Clements will meet you at the station. That's very kind of him. I think Victoria is old enough for me to speak frankly to you both. In the long run this sort of thing doesn't help you to be together. It's just painful for everybody.

Paula I'm only fucking human. Don't you use words like that, Victoria.

Victoria Words like human?

Miranda You're going back to the Clements' house, Victoria. Do you understand why?

Victoria I don't want to go back. They eat funny.

Paula She doesn't want to go back. What you don't understand is that you can't keep taking things away from people, it fucks up their heads.

Miranda Would you wait outside for a minute, Victoria. There's a chair by the door.

Paula Go on, love. Take your comic.

Victoria This is my new T-shirt, Pocahontas. (*She exits.*)

Miranda What happened?

Paula It just seemed right at the time. We had a nice day.

Then you think, why has it got to end? Who says?

Miranda I do understand. It is hard. But it's no solution, is it? Running back to London with her. (*Pause.*) I would like your asurance that it won't happen again.

Paula It won't happen again.

Miranda When I discuss your case with the team, I'll emphasize that this was an isolated incident.

Paula Thanks. (*She lights a cigarette.*)

Miranda There is another thing.

Paula Not the pissing group again?

Miranda No.

Paula I haven't sorted out my GCSEs if that's what you mean.

Miranda No, it's about money.

Paula Oh, yes, I've got your money. Thanks.

She gives Miranda twenty quid.

Miranda What I was wondering was where you got the money? For the cinema, Victoria's train fare, the T-shirt?

Paula What do you mean?

Miranda I was wondering where you got the money?

Paula What?

Miranda The money. I really can't overlook it. I'm asking.

Paula I couldn't go down there with no money, Miranda. (*Pause.*) I'm not ashamed. I took ten minutes out of my life and I gave a man a blow job.

Miranda I'm not judging you. I understand that women get desperate and as a last resort . . .

Paula That's your O-level prostitution talking.

Miranda It's a serious matter.

Paula It's nothing. It's easy. I start off with my hand. I only put it in my mouth for the last bit. When it's hard.

Miranda I don't want the details.

Paula I thought that would be one of the perks.

Miranda On the contrary.

Paula It's a sort of social work in a way. I provide the service their wives can't handle.

Miranda Do you take these clients home?

Paula What?

Miranda Do you take them home?

Paula No. I do not.

Miranda I don't know if I believe that, Paula.

Paula I wouldn't take them home if Victoria was there, would I?

Miranda You are a bright, capable person, Paula, and you have to start believing in the future. In yourself.

Paula Or what?

Miranda It's up to you. I can only support you if you want my support. Or you jeopardize everything. You'll need to explain to Victoria about going back. I'll see you at the group, Paula.

Pause. Paula opens the door.

Paula Victoria.

Victoria comes in.

You go back to the Clements. It's not for ever. Just till
Mum gets back on her feet. It won't be long.

Victoria How long, Mum?

Paula Not long I said, didn't I? Now, get your jacket on.

Victoria puts her jacket on.

Victoria How long, Mum?

Miranda takes them to the door. They exit.

SCENE EIGHT

*Roger sits alone. He does not work. Emma enters
Miranda and Roger's front room.*

Emma It's me.

Roger Miranda's working late.

Emma walks about restlessly.

Do you want to take off your coat?

Emma Oh my God, I've done something terrible.

Roger I'm sure it was nothing too terrible.

Emma I feel awful. It's hard having Miranda as a friend.
It's hard to live up to.

Roger I know. I know. Don't worry.

Emma I do worry, Roger, I do. You don't know what I
am. Miranda doesn't know. If she knew I don't think
she'd like me.

Roger I think you're being very hard on yourself. I'm
sure you haven't done anything much.

Emma How would you know?

Roger Well, I don't actually know. But I do know you, so I was happy to conclude that I was sure that you hadn't done anything much.

Emma Bollocks.

Roger Would you like a drink, Emma?

Emma What I hate is sure people. People who are always so bloody sure. (*She takes off her top.*)

Roger What are you doing?

Emma I'm surprising you. I'm showing you that you don't know anybody. You don't know what they've done and you couldn't begin to guess.

Roger Please put on your jumper.

Emma No. I'm going to sit here in my bra and have a fag and give myself cancer. Any objections? Because you're a decent and good person, Roger, you think everyone else is decent and good too. But we're not. Some of us are murky.

Roger Emma.

Emma No. I've done something. Something sickening and if you try to calm me down I'll scream. You'd never understand, Roger.

Roger I might.

Emma No, you're too . . .

Roger Too . . .?

Emma Flattened. Sorry.

Roger Flattened?

Emma Don't take it the wrong way.

Roger Flattened?

Emma It's not a bad thing to be. It's safe at least.

Pause.

Roger I did something.

Emma What? You did?

Roger Yes. I don't know how it happened. She's a student. She's twenty years old. She's French, from the border with Belgium, actually. She's in my Hegelian thought module. Anyway, I found her attractive. It was the end of term and I'd had a bottle of wine. It was the end of term party and we . . . and we . . .

Emma Try to breathe and talk at the same time, Roger.

Roger The terrible thing is it was when Miranda was sick. That's the thing. When she was sick. How wretched.

Emma Have you done anything since?

Roger No, no. I haven't. I swear I haven't.

Emma Oh well, forget it.

Roger Forget it?

Emma It's nothing really. Christ, on Thursday I went home with a strange man who tied me up, wore a hood and called me obscene names while I spat at his navel.

Roger Really?

Emma Safe sex.

They look at each other.

Roger We crept into the gardens. It was dark. When I felt her skin it was a shock. Such young skin and mine seemed old. I seemed on the edge of being irretrievably old. And I reached out and held on. A pang. Unbearably fantastic.

Emma Well, now we're partners in crime. Have a cigarette.

She offers him one, he hesitates.

Don't worry. If you catch alight I'm good in an emergency.

He moves towards her.

No kissing.

SCENE NINE

The group.

Miranda Do you want to talk about what happened to you last week, Paula?

Paula I kidnapped my own kid. It lasted two hours. I was bollocked. The end. By Paula.

Miranda It must have been difficult leaving her.

Paula Yes, it was. Victoria wet herself on the train home.

Miranda That must have been upsetting. Do you want to explore that with the group?

Nicola I could be Victoria if you like.

Paula No you can't. You're nothing like Victoria. She's sensible and charismatic.

Miranda I think what we're saying is that there's a space for you to do that, Paula, if you want it.

Paula No thank you.

Miranda arranges two chairs as an interview room.

Miranda Something different. Nicola, you're interviewing Paula for a job. Paula's got an interview coming up. For a cashier.

Paula I won't get it.

They begin.

Nicola Do sit down.

Paula sits.

Nicola Now, Paula.

Paula Yes.

Nicola Can you tell me a little about your past work experience?

Paula I haven't got any. Do you mind if I smoke?

Nicola We do have a no-smoking policy in this building.

Paula Smoking helps me think.

Nicola We do have a lot of applications for this post.

Paula Yes, but that's not because it's a good job. It's because people can't afford to be choosy. It's not something you'd lie in bed dreaming about.

Nicola Our staff tell us they're quite happy. We have a very good staff–management relationship.

Paula But you don't know what they say behind your back.

Nicola What do they say behind our back?

Paula I'm not going to tell you, am I? It might prejudice my chances.

Miranda Do you want this job, Paula?

Paula Yes.

Miranda Well, just try to keep focused on that. How did it go from your point of view, Nicola?

Nicola Well, not too good.

Miranda Would you have given her the job?

Pause.

Nicola Probably not. Depends if we were desperate.

Paula Desperate?

Miranda Try swapping over.

Nicola 'knocks' on the door.

Paula Just a minute. (*to Miranda*) That's what they do. To make you feel more nervous. Come in. Yes, you must be Ranjit.

Nicola No, Paula.

Paula Oh, yes, of course. I don't expect you've got qualifications or you wouldn't be here. Now, why do you want to come and work for us?

Nicola Well, it's about my life.

Paula What about your life?

Nicola I want another chance. There's certain things I want to be able to do in my life and getting a job is all part of that. I really want a job. Then I can break all my old patterns. I can start to restructure my life. I'll go to work in the morning. I'll probably make a few friends at work. New people. So I won't be miserable going. I'll look forward to seeing them. And maybe some of the customers. We might have chats sometimes. And at the end of the day I will be tired but it won't be the sort of tired when you're sitting around all day watching bad TV and smoking. It will feel like a positive tiredness. And then I'll go and pick up my little girl from school. And then I'll cook her tea and we'll talk. We'll talk about our day. I'll say the things that happened to me and she'll say the things that happened to her. Sometimes I might have to help her with something. A problem that's cropped up. And that will make me feel glad because I'll have been able to help. I'll have been able to do something to help someone I really love.

Paula That was brilliant!

Miranda Nicola. Well done.

Paula Fucking excellent.

Nicola sits down.

Still, if you said that in real life they'd think you were off your case.

Miranda I think they'd sympathize with the spirit of it. What do you think, Emma? Would you give her the job?

Emma What? Oh. Yes. I suppose so.

Miranda Is there something you'd like to talk to us about?

Emma Yes. Wish me luck. I'm going into the occasion-card business.

Miranda So you're giving up on the painting?

Emma Yes. After decades of being ignored by the art world I've finally taken the hint.

Miranda Emma is a wonderful painter. She did a portrait of us together once. She called it sisters.

Nicola That's fantastic. There must have been a real feeling of sisterhood then. Back then.

Emma Oh, yes. It was sisterhood this and sisterhood that.

Paula I don't talk to my sister. She's a cow.

Miranda Well, there are often complicated dynamics that arise between siblings.

Paula She's a fucking cow. There's something evil inside her that's always been there. She wouldn't have Victoria when I went away. That's why I'm in this mess.

Emma That's what's so terrifying. What's inside you that you never knew about. Our next-door neighbours had a tortoise. Something about the size of a shoe used to set it off. They'd all be sitting there on a Sunday with their G and Ts, all chatting and laughing and then one of them would look down and scream because Finbar was shagging their plimsole. There'd be a cry and a clattering sound as he was booted off and bounced across the York stone.

Nicola That doesn't sound normal to me. Maybe they disturbed his hibernation patterns.

Emma He was obeying something primitive.

Miranda His deep attraction to footwear. What are we really talking about here, Emma?

Emma Pets. Something was driving that tortoise.

Paula He was a randy little bugger.

Emma A natural force.

Nicola Tortoises have bad eyes. It was probably all a mistake.

Emma I mean, what's disgusting and what isn't and who decides?

Nicola Anything that hurts someone is disgusting.

Paula Anything that takes longer than five minutes to clear up.

Miranda I think people know that nothing done with love is disgusting.

Paula So if Finbar loved that plimsole he's OK. If he just fancied it he's a pervert.

Emma You see, people can get strait-jacketed into what's considered a normal sex life and they never feel free to experiment.

Miranda Are you worried because you're sleeping with Alan's coat?

Emma What?

Paula Whose coat?

Miranda It hardly qualifies you for inclusion in the category of sexual peversion.

Emma You didn't have to mention the coat. Now everyone knows I'm a weak and stupid person who sleeps with a man's coat because that's all she can manage.

Miranda Nobody thinks that, Emma.

Emma That's the thing with these groups. You come along with all these expectations and somehow they make you feel worse. Smaller.

Miranda Is that really your experience of them, Emma?

Emma Once I was in a consciousness-raising group and we passed a waste-paper bin round and we all tipped our make-up into it.

Paula What for?

Emma Make-up was oppressive.

Paula But it makes you look a fuck of a lot better.

Nicola (*to Emma*) I think that's brilliant.

Emma That's because I haven't finished. Later I sneaked back and got my mascara.

Paula Good for you.

Nicola Why?

Emma I have small eyes.

Miranda You have perfectly fine eyes.

Emma You have perfectly fine eyes. I have small eyes. I was supposed to pretend I had perfectly fine eyes and that I felt fine but what I really felt was ugly and stupid for minding about it. But that was the last thing you were ever allowed to admit to. It was all like that. Lots of pretending.

Miranda I had no idea you felt like that. I never did.

Emma It was like a sort of conspiracy. You were shut out if you said anything wrong.

Paula Women are bitchy.

Nicola There's an excellent book you should read: *Man Made Language*.

Paula You know how to enjoy yourself, Nick.

Miranda Emma. This is unbelievable.

Emma No it isn't. I'm still afraid to say things.

Miranda There's nothing you can't talk about here. If you want to sell birthday cards you should discuss it here. Really face what you're leaving behind.

Emma All right. In the past I wanted to be an artist. A very good woman artist. I felt I had a mission. Because behind us were centuries of women who had been denied the opportunity to express themselves. Whose talent had been stamped out.

Nicola And what happened?

Emma Time sort of went on. I had a few small exhibitions. One in Brighton, one in a small gallery in North London under some railway arches. I used to paint in a little room at the top of the house and it became harder and harder to climb the stairs. I drank at lunchtimes and napped in the afternoon. I did a bit of teaching. Then this thing called conceptual art happened. There were exhibits entitled 'Condom Hardening under Glass'. I was lost, I suppose. What it took me a while to understand was that I didn't have any talent.

Nicola Yes, yes, you did. I'm sure you did.

Emma No. You have to have the sort of passion a mother has for a child. I never felt that. I was just average. So you see, I was sort of fooled.

Miranda We were a bit naive. Your work was resisted because it challenged the status quo.

Nicola That must be it.

Emma I had an idea of myself that was nothing like who I was.

Miranda I loved your paintings. Your painting, Emma. That one of us. Take it to a gallery.

Emma I can't. They won't be interested.

Miranda Take it to a gallery run by a woman.

Emma That's no guarantee of anything.

Miranda Try.

Emma There's nothing I'd like more than to be good. But I'm not good enough, I'm not. And it's taken a lot to get to this point.

Nicola Why are you arguing?

Emma Maybe everything was a big fucking mistake. Have you ever thought of that, Miranda?

Nicola Why are you shouting at Miranda?

Miranda It wasn't a mistake. It's all right, Nicola.

Emma Just do this and this and all the good talented things inside you will come out. Abandon the life of your mothers. Well, I did and now I've got nothing. No career, no husband, no child. Nothing's turned out the way it was supposed to.

Pause.

Miranda Perhaps things haven't turned out the way we wanted. Maybe the world we imagined was so miraculous that it's not possible that it could exist. I remember waking up one morning. There were a group of us squatting a building we wanted for a women's refuge. It was freezing. I could hear birds and this feeling shot through me. At first I didn't know what it was and then I realized it was joy. Just joy. I thought, I am where I want to be. I am doing totally what I want to do and believe I should be doing and it is completely liberating. No energy wasted in doubt or despair. A moment of absolute certainty. You choose to go on acting on that faith because you know it's the best thing you've got.

Emma I can't come any more. Don't try to make me stay.

Before Emma can leave Nicola begins.

Nicola Dad? Dad? Are you asleep?

(*as Geoff*) I wasn't asleep.

Nicola You shouldn't have waited up for me, Dad, if you're tired.

(*as Geoff*) I was thinking about Greece. It's a beautiful

286

country, Nicola. Full of decayed classicism. The islands are especially beautiful, white chalky houses and a deep blue sea.

Nicola Sounds beautiful.

(*as Geoff*) I said that, Nicola. You're supposed to think of a conversation opener now, Nicola, like 'When was the last time you visited Greece?'or 'How long does the boat take from Athens to the islands?'

Nicola I think I'll go to bed now, Dad.

(*as Geoff*) I went to Greece with your mum, Nick. We were a bit hippyish. I've got the photo. I looked funny, didn't I? Sandals, beard, flappy-bottomed trousers.

Nicola I want to do a bit of reading before I crash out. Exams in a month.

(*as Geoff*) Do you think of her much, Nick?

Nicola Yes.

(*as Geoff*) Your poor mum. Poor Deirdre. We thought it was just tiredness. It was when the nausea started that a bell rang for me. A bell, low, threatening thunder.

Nicola Dad.

(*as Geoff*) Terrible pain.

Nicola Dad.

(*as Geoff*) Bottomless.

Nicola Dad.

(*as Geoff*) She was in pain at the end. Couldn't swallow. Had to spit into a bowl. A tree grew out of her tongue. Very rare.

Nicola Dad. Stop it.

(*as Geoff*) Cancer. Drank myself to oblivion. Yum, yum.

Nicola Feel sick.

(*as Geoff*) A cold coming we had of it. Just the worst time of year for a journey and such a long journey.

Nicola gags. Bends over.

Miranda Nicola? It's all right. I'm here. I'm here. You're OK.

Miranda puts her arm round Nicola. Sits down with her. Paula lights a cigarette. Emma stands watching.

Paula I never meant what I said. About you being Victoria.

Emma Poor Nicola.

Miranda You're OK. You're OK.

Paula I've been to Greece. 1987. With Victoria's dad before he went back to his wife. We went to Mykonos. Fantastic. All night dancing. The men are very good-looking. We had beer for breakfast. We used to have it looking at the sea. The sound of the sea is very soothing. Just listening to the sea. That's because that's what a baby hears inside its mother. It hears a sound like the sound of the sea. A shush shush sound. But really it's the blood going in and out of the mother's heart. It's comforting. That's why we like the sound of the sea, apparently.

Miranda There's a story that the earth gave birth to the sea. That the earth was the most powerful goddess and the sea came from her belly.

Nicola I like that story.

Emma sits with group.

Act Two

SCENE ONE

Roger is standing by the phone. He hears Miranda come downstairs. He hurriedly sits down. Miranda enters.

Roger Emma was here.

Miranda What did she want?

Roger She wanted to see you. We talked about Alan mostly.

Miranda Emma. She's always managed to pick rotten men.

Roger Has she? Alan's not that bad, is he?

Miranda He had a thin veneer of PC. Underneath he was a latent Chef of the Year.

Roger He's opening a new restaurant apparently. Alan always seemed to be drifting. We used to think he was a bit of a joke. Now he must be gloating.

Miranda Would you be gloating if you were Alan? Alan isn't writing a book on Hegel.

Roger No.

Miranda You're making a lasting contribution, Roger. Alan is making crêpes.

Roger The thing is, I'd be gloating if I was Alan. I'd be thinking, 'Poor old Roger. His yeast isn't rising. He's got a paunch and a writing block and I've got two restaurants and I'm minting it in.'

Miranda He's making money, Roger. What's that? It's just money. We've got much more than he's got. We're committed to living our lives with some sort of vision.

Roger In the morning I have leg cramps. What do you think that is?

Miranda I don't know. Are you feeling all right?

Roger I've just been sitting here drinking too much wine. Feeling sorry for myself. (*Pause.*) Why am I writing a book on Hegel?

Miranda You must know that.

Roger Because he said, 'History is the progress of reason in the world.' The other day it just slipped my mind. I sat there for three solid hours. I only wrote two sentences.

Miranda Maybe they were key sentences.

Roger Then I scribbled them out again.

Miranda Well things fell apart a bit when I was sick but I'm here now. (*Pause.*) All this stuff about Alan, I don't know where it's come from. And your book. You've been planning that for years. I was thinking. You were so sweet to me when I was ill. Force-feeding me vitamin Cs.

Roger Without vitamin C the body can't process any other vitamins.

Miranda I think we should plan a holiday. What was the name of that place we went to in France?

Roger Miranda? (*Pause.*) In fact it's funny that we've been talking about Alan because actually I've just been speaking to him on the phone.

Miranda Did he phone you?

Roger Well, one of us phoned one of us. For a chat. You know. Anyway, he asked me to come along to his group.

Miranda What group's that?

Roger His group. His men's group.

Miranda Oh.

Roger Yes. Yes. That's what I thought.

Miranda What did you think?

Roger Well, I thought 'oh' like you. Anyway I said I'd go. But I probably won't. The thing is, I have to make up my mind in the next five minutes. It's a weekend retreat. I've packed a bag. (*He pulls a bag out from behind a chair.*) But it doesn't mean I'm definitely going.

Miranda I thought you wanted to see a film tomorrow.

Roger Well, I did. I do. I did. Alan said some weird things.

Miranda What things?

Roger Men mustn't be afraid of being men.

Miranda What did he mean?

Roger I don't know. Ha ha. It's really a suspect and ridiculous statement with absolutely no attempt at historical contextualizing. Ha ha.

Miranda Very Alan.

Roger Yes, yes, precisely. Very Alan. I have to bring some tough boots, an outdoor winter jacket and my favourite poem.

Miranda What's that?

Roger 'The Jabberwocky'. Funnily enough that was Alan's choice when he was initiated.

Miranda Are you being initiated?

Roger No, no, no. I'm not even necessarily going.

Miranda It seems like you are.

Roger Am I? I just think I need a break. To get out of London. Clear my head. There are so many things going on in my head.

Miranda You could have talked to me about them.

Roger I know, I know. The thing is, I said I'd go.

Miranda I can tell you now what you'll think of it.

Roger A lot of silly, hung-up men. I thought I could look at it as a sociological experience. I've taken the tin opener. We drive down to Bournemouth tonight. Our hotel overlooks the seafront. We get non-seasonal rates. The idea is we get to see the dawn.

Miranda Well, happy dawn.

Roger Right. Right. (*He picks up his bag.*) What am I doing? I don't deserve you. I don't even want to go. I just said I would to Alan. On the spur of the moment.

Miranda Go on.

Roger Bye. You do understand. I'd rather be here with you.

He exits. Miranda stands uncertainly.

SCENE TWO

Paula, alone, outside, a phone box.

Paula Hello? Hello? Miranda? It's me. Paula. A phone box on the Old Kent Road. It's a sort of tramp's toilet. I'm standing in fossilized tramp's pee. If I pass out halfway through you'll know why. I've just popped out from

work. I don't want them listening. It's all right. So. Now
I'm a taxpayer can I have my kid back? What? Sorry, a
lorry. It's pissing down. It's like being in a sort of human
car wash. So what did the team say? I know, I know. I
can't wait until tomorrow. What's the decision? I wasn't
expecting anything. Fuck those fucking lorries. Yes, yes. I
heard. I heard. Why? I am settled into a routine. I've done
a week. Yeah. Yeah. Stick to the plan. Another month. I
know it's a process. What? Yeah, yeah. I'm OK. Me
money's run out.

She puts down the phone. Stands. Exits. Sound of rain.

SCENE THREE

*Greenwich park. A hilltop. Remnants of a small picnic.
Paula looks tired. Nicola lies a short distance away, reading a textbook.*

Victoria Mum?

Paula What?

Victoria Say 'fuzzy duck' very fast.

Paula No.

Victoria Why not?

Paula You know why not.

Victoria Mum?

Paula What?

Victoria What's an airwave?

Paula Does it matter? I'm having a rest. (*Pause.*) Here.
Have a doughnut.

Victoria What sort?

Paula How many sorts are there? If you want one have one. If not . . .

Victoria Are they from work again?

Paula Yes.

Victoria Grungenuts. Is Nicola a grunge? I'm going to ask her.

Paula Don't ask her.

Victoria What does your shop sell?

Paula Everything all the time and it expects me to be there.

Victoria Does it sell buildings?

Paula Don't be stupid.

Victoria You said everything.

Paula There's no need to be stupid.

Victoria Patrick and Isobel don't say stupid.

Paula What do they say then?

Victoria Hasn't thoroughly comprehended.

Paula That means stupid.

Victoria It doesn't.

Paula It means stupid. Stupid. (*Pause.*) I didn't mean that. I've been really looking forward to today. To have you come down for the day. It's my day off. I get Wednesdays off.

Victoria Why?

Paula Instead of Sundays.

Victoria Patrick doesn't work on Sundays. Or Saturdays.

Paula Well, banks don't open then, do they?

Victoria No. We're going on holiday.

Paula What?

Victoria To Lyon.

Paula Where?

Victoria Isobel is half French.

Paula Fucking hell.

Victoria *Je m'appelle Victoria. Et je habite à Sussex.*

Paula All right. All right.

Victoria They're going to ask you if it's OK.

Paula Have a doughnut.

Victoria *Non merci.*

Paula Do you want a doughnut, Nick?

Nicola Oh, no thanks.

Paula Don't then. No one have one. (*She picks up the doughnuts and empties the bag.*) They are obviously crap.

Nicola They looked like really nice ones to me.

Victoria She's in a bad mood.

Nicola I'm sure she's not. Not today.

Victoria It's because of Lyon.

Nicola Is that a friend from school?

Victoria No, it's the third largest city in France.

Nicola Oh.

Victoria You don't want me to go.

Paula Go where you like. I can't stop you. You go to Lyon and don't worry about me slogging me guts out in some poxy job.

Victoria It's not my fault it's a poxy job.

Nicola It's not a bad job. It's a positive step. Isn't it, Paula?

Paula Yeah, all right, Nicola. Go for a run, Victoria.

Victoria Why?

Paula You've got too much energy.

Victoria Running's boring.

Paula Run to that tree and back, go on.

Victoria No. You do it.

Paula I'm warning you.

Victoria I want to go to Lyon.

Paula Shut up about Lyon.

Victoria I hate you.

Paula Don't say that, you little cow.

Nicola begins to pick up the doughnuts and put them back in the bag.

Nicola Guess what. This morning Dad boarded up the windows. He wanted to make the windows safe. So he took all these bits of wood from crates and things and hammered them over the windows. Bang, bang.

Victoria What for?

Nicola He said there was a storm coming. The sort Noah had in the Bible.

Paula Remind him he lives in Peckham.

Nicola Yes.

Victoria He sounds like a loony.

Paula Victoria.

Victoria That's what you said.

Paula I did not.

Nicola Don't worry. Lunatic is a bit of an old-fashioned word. Now we tend to use the term mentally ill or mentally unstable. Everyone gets a bit fed up with their job sometimes, Victoria. It's natural. (*to Paula*) Thanks for letting me come. I needed to get out.

Paula You wouldn't do it, would you?

Nicola What?

Paula My job.

Nicola Well, I wouldn't want to do it for ever.

Paula Well, how long would you do it for?

Nicola For as long as I needed to. I mean it would be part of a plan. A longer-term plan. You have to think of where you'll be in five years or so. That's what Miranda says.

Paula So where will I be in five years?

Nicola I don't know. Where do you envisage you'll be?

Paula I envisage myself as older and smoking more fags.

Nicola What about good things?

Paula What about them?

Nicola Yes, what about them?

Paula God, this is a fucking depressing conversation.

Nicola It only seems depressing at the start but if we carried on things would seem better.

Paula What I hate is waking up every morning in temporary accommodation with no teabags. I'm twenty-nine, I want to feel good when I wake up. You make a plan, you think, 'Great, I'll stick to that.' Only it's too dull or it's too hard. No one's giving anything to me. The third largest city in France. I didn't fucking know that, did you? The thing is, Nick, I know I should want her to go. You know, love it that she gets the opportunity. That's how I should feel, but I don't.

Nicola One visit to France is worth months in the classroom. For learning the language.

Victoria Mum. Where will I go if they go on holiday? Will I be on my own?

Paula Come here. Give me a hug.

Victoria gives her a hug.

Tighter. Tighter.

Victoria hugs her tighter.

Till it hurts. You go on holiday, that's fine by me. Just fine. (*Pause.*) I've got friends of my own remember.

Victoria Who?

Paula Friends.

Victoria Michael? (*Pause.*) You went to prison.

Paula Ten out of ten, Victoria.

Victoria Mum.

Paula Yes?

Victoria I've done something.

Paula What?

Victoria I've wet myself.

Paula You haven't?

Nicola Oh dear, never mind. I've got a tissue.

She begins to wipe Victoria's legs.

Victoria Wart wart schlobb tomato. That's how lunatics speak. Amble scramble bum beehive doughnut burp.

SCENE FOUR

Roger at home. He has just come in from a jog and is still in his jogging clothes. Emma enters. She has been drinking.

Emma I've come to give Miranda this. (*She holds her painting wrapped in a blanket.*)

Roger Right.

Emma So how are you?

Roger Fine, fine. Splendid.

Emma You don't look splendid, you look puffy. Still fucking that French girl?

Roger Is that the painting Miranda mentioned?

Emma Don't you love Miranda?

Roger Yes.

Emma Then why are you doing it?

Roger I'm not doing it.

Emma Yes you are. You're making love with a twenty-year-old from the border with Belgium.

Roger It's something I intend putting an end to in the near future.

Emma Really?

Roger Yes, at present it's not something I'm quite in control of. It's like Shakespeare said, a sort of madness, or as the romantics would have it, a fever.

Emma Thank you, professor. Do you know what I think? (*She swigs from her bottle.*) I think you're like a boil that's popped. There's all this stuff in you and for years you've pretended to be as antiseptic as hell and now in late middle-age it's pushed its way to the surface and burst all over your life.

Roger Charming.

Emma I think you're despicable.

Roger I'm the first to admit I've behaved badly.

Emma Pus-y, disgusting.

Roger I took advantage of Miranda's sickness.

Emma What would Hegel say?

Roger He'd be very disappointed.

Emma I've a good mind to write him a letter. Put a spoke up his zeitgeist.

Roger Have we got a safe word?

Emma How about punt?

Roger Punt?

Emma Any objections?

Roger The means of transport or the currency?

Emma Take your pick. It's a free country. (*She takes out* *some rope and begins to tie Roger up.*)

Roger The means of transport.

Emma continues to tie Roger.

Emma It's not the sort of thing she's interested in.

Roger Who?

Emma The woman at the gallery, Roger. What's the matter, aren't you bloody listening?

Roger Yes, I'm your slave.

Emma I took my courage in both hands and asked her if she'd like to see my other work.

Roger And?

Emma Nope.

Roger I see. Oh dear.

Emma Oh deary, deary, dear. She's interested in African artefacts and postmodern installations.

Roger You can try somewhere else. You are the mistress of figurative representation.

Emma That's what sickens me about you people. Your horrible cheery optimism. You bob along in a sort of sickly dream world.

Roger We've only got an hour.

Emma It's a lovely painting. Miranda and me. We look all shiny. And there's some lilies.

Roger An hour might be pushing it.

Emma When I got up this morning I felt hopeful. I am such a dupe.

Roger That was one gallery, Emma. There must be thousands. Perhaps this isn't a good time.

Emma For what?

Roger To do this. Um . . . this.

Emma Why can't you say it?

Roger I don't know. It's not coming out.

Emma S and M, Roger. You people can't even say it.

Roger Why do you keep saying that? 'You people' like that.

Emma Because I'm referring to yourself and Miranda. You people. The boil people. (*She goes over to Roger, ruffles his hair. Unzips his jogging top. Sits down opposite him with her bottle.*) The title of this work is boiling point.

Roger Emma?

No reply.

What are you doing?

Emma I'm just sitting here.

Roger Aren't you going to . . .?

Emma What?

Roger Start. What are you going to do to me, Emma?

Emma Don't get your hopes up, Roger. I'm going to wait till Mummy gets here and then I'm going to let her deal with it.

Roger Very good. Very good.

Emma What?

Roger This is a twist in the game. It's a twist in the game. (*Pause.*) You're not really going to let Miranda walk in on this? What is the point of that?

Emma Communication. You're a sort of living picture. I want Miranda to see the bollocks.

Roger This is about the painting. You're angry and upset because your painting was rejected and you feel hurt. Now you want to hurt someone in return. (*Pause.*) Miranda is working very hard at the moment. Too hard. But if you feel you want to destroy her, go ahead.

Emma You're destroying her too. Fucking about.

Roger But I'm going to stop. Miranda means more to me than anything else in the world. What's happening between us, Emma, is a sort of aberration. It's not us. Not who we are. It's a sort of hiccup.

Emma You always put such a happy sheen on things. But aren't we an ugly pair doing an ugly thing?

Roger Emma. I think you may be a little disturbed today. Today may not be a good day to do anything rash.

Emma has another drink.

Untie me please, Emma.

Emma Give me an explanation and I'll untie you. Make us all nice again and I'll be nice.

Roger We are nice. We are.

Emma Prove it to me. Oh, and listen. There's Mummy's car. I can hear the brakes go squealy squealy. Mummy needs some brake oil.

Roger Punt, Emma.

Emma Punt yourself.

Roger Punt, punt, punt.

Emma I want her to see.

Roger Fucking punt!

Emma Mr Boily's going to pop!

Roger Untie me, Emma.

Emma Emma can't do knots.

Roger That's childish, Emma. (*He struggles with his ropes but has no success.*) Please, Emma.

Emma You've got about forty-five seconds.

Roger Forty-five seconds.

Emma Make everything all right. This all right.

Pause.

Roger (*very fast*) Well. I think we have to look at things as a tube. A sort of tube. Like a toothpaste tube. Now, in order to survive, man, woman, has to employ reason. Reason is by definition good because it seeks the optimum conditions for survival. Those conditions are peace, co-operation and plenty. Now, as we know, man, woman, has a dark side, and that – here we have to give Freud due credit – is suppressed for the benefit of civilization. But this dark side sometimes has to be released in small quantities like toothpaste being squeezed from a bulging tube. So . . . so . . . this is what is squeezed out to relieve the pressure. And that must be a good thing. Ultimately re-inforcing the very fabric of social cohesion.

Emma I didn't understand a word of that.

Roger Emma, it's very simple . . . a tube . . .

Emma Is that the sort of thing you tell your students? You make it up as you go along. No, Roger, no. It didn't work. I'm sorry. Tube or no tube look at us, what we've been doing. You can't make it decent or useful.

Roger (*very upset*) Emma, Emma, I don't know what's been happening to me. I'm frightened all the time. What have I been doing for the last ten years? I feel like I must have been asleep. Where have they gone? I feel like I've woken up and my life's just gone by and I never noticed. And what's ahead of me? A sort of blackness. I'm not really sleeping, I'm drinking. I'm scared, Emma, scared.

Emma is moved.

Emma Poor Roger.

Miranda's voice, off.

Miranda Hello!

Roger and Emma freeze. Then Emma grabs the blanket that covers the painting and flings it over Roger so that his ties cannot be seen.
Miranda enters.

Miranda Why are you all wrapped up?

Roger I was asleep, I was asleep and Emma came in.

Emma I brought the painting for you.

Miranda No luck?

Roger Don't let's go into all that.

Miranda I'm just asking.

Emma No. She didn't like it. So I thought you might like it. You're always going on about it.

Miranda I think it's wonderful, that's why. You can't just give up, Emma. It's so like you to give up after one try. Isn't it, Roger?

Roger No.

Emma Just leave me alone.

Miranda I'm only keeping on about it because I know how much support you need.

Roger Just leave her alone.

Miranda What's this? Some sort of conspiracy?

Roger No, no.

Miranda I just don't want you slipping back, Emma.

Emma Slipping back?

Miranda Yes.

Emma I haven't just slipped, Miranda, I've plunged.

Roger Stop!

Emma We both have.

She pulls blanket off Roger, revealing his ties.

Roger Christ. (*He falls off the sofa and begins to try to wriggle across the floor.*) Ah! (*He stops, jerks, shakes, goes unconscious.*)

Miranda Roger?

His ties are revealed. Miranda stares at him.

Emma Better get him some water. Quickly.

Miranda exits.
Emma begins to untie Roger.

Sorry, Roger. (*She struggles with ropes.*) I tied these a bit tight. Maybe, maybe in a few years all this will have blown over. Maybe, maybe then we can even be friends again.

Roger sighs.
Miranda re-enters.

He's still breathing.

Roger opens his eyes.

Roger Miranda?

Miranda Don't try to sit up.

Roger I'm OK. I'm OK.

Miranda You may have had a heart attack.

Roger No, no. I haven't.

Miranda I'll phone for an ambulance. Don't try to move.

Roger I don't want an ambulance. (*He gets up.*)

Miranda What are you doing?

Roger I'm going to change. (*He exits.*)

Emma I can explain, Miranda.

Miranda Don't.

Emma But I want to. I think, right from the beginning, from the very first time we met, we've been building up to this. This moment.

Miranda I don't want to listen to this.

Emma I always looked up to you and wanted to be like you. But I was different. You knew that but it made you powerful to feel you had to help me. You were full of theories and the right way to be and in the end it began to feel like criticism. Then I secretly began to hate you. And that's why. With Roger.

Miranda I don't know you. Please go now.

Emma I'll wait with you. Make sure everything's OK.

Miranda No. Go.

Emma hesitates, then decides to go.

Emma I'll take the picture, shall I?

Miranda No. Leave the picture.

Roger comes back.

Emma Well, goodbye. (*She exits.*)

Roger It wasn't my heart.

Miranda What was it then?

Roger It's hard to explain. (*Pause.*) I think I was passing from one state into another.

Miranda What?

Roger Yes. A sort of shamanic process. Native Americans are very familiar with it.

Miranda Don't talk shit, Roger.

Roger Don't dismiss it, Miranda, you know nothing about it. We have parallels in our own culture. Illness. People get ill at times of traumatic change.

Miranda You shit. With my best friend.

Roger Look.

Miranda In that disgusting way.

Roger I am sorry. Truly sorry.

Miranda In my house. Did you ever think about me? What it might do to me? Did you hate me too? Did you want to hurt me?

Roger No. No. That was the last thing I wanted to do.

Miranda I try. I try really hard. I work hard.

Roger I know. I know.

Miranda So why?

Roger I don't know.

Miranda You must know. There's always an answer.

Roger I don't know.

Miranda I'm still tired. I'm tired all the time, Roger. But I don't want to give in to it. And now this.

Roger I know. I know.

Miranda You prick.

Roger Miranda. Don't call me that.

Miranda Prick. You spineless prick.

Roger You have a fear of masculinity, Miranda.

Miranda Oh God.

Roger It's meant over the years that I have had to suppress certain male elements of my psyche.

Miranda No, no.

Roger Because I loved you and wanted to be with you, I have suppressed these elements but at a cost. A cost to me as a man.

Miranda You've done a bit of washing up. You've refrained from using the word cunt. You read *The Bell Jar*.

Roger I think there was a necessity in all that. It was an historical moment that I feel proud to have participated in but the moment has passed.

Miranda Nothing's passed.

Roger I think you've got stuck, Miranda. The world's moved on.

Miranda You've given up, Roger. That's all. Nothing's moved on. You've shrunk into the world of Roger. What's important to you is pleasuring yourself and when that gets boring and narrow you have to think up more and more perverse and degrading ways to do it. Will you be able to squeeze another drop of sensation out of your tired, sated body?

Roger You see, that's the thing. How you see me. But really I'm at a sort of peak. I have to start looking at myself dynamically. Being with people who look at me dynamically. As Alan said, I could still have children. A whole new start.

Miranda I'd hate to think I'd been holding you back.

Roger I'm going.

Miranda Going?

Roger To stay with Alan. He says there's plenty of room. (*Pause.*) Believe it or not I didn't plan all this. It just happened. I'll get my things.

Miranda You've settled for so little, Roger. How could you?

He exits. She is left alone. She calls after him.

How could you? (*She puts the picture somewhere prominent and looks at it.*)

SCENE FIVE

Paula and Miranda. Miranda's house. Around lie boxes. Miranda is packing up Roger's things.

Paula It's urgent.

Miranda doesn't respond.

It's urgent, Miranda. I ran out. I ran out from work.

Miranda It's Sunday. Isn't it your day off?

Paula No. Wednesdays. I ran out. You have to phone them, Miranda. I know I'm close to getting Victoria back. Make some excuse. Just say something about social services. I had an urgent appointment, something like that.

Miranda You explain to them, Paula.

Paula I can't. There's this cunt who's the manager and he wants me on the night shift. I told him to fuck off and then I came here. He can't do that, can he, Miranda? What about Victoria? (*Pause.*) I think you should phone him now. 407 4007. I have to go back. If you walk out of a job you lose your benefits.

Miranda does so. It takes a lot of effort. Paula prompts her.

Miranda Hello, I'm phoning about Paula . . . yes, yes. Her social worker. Miranda Hurst. Yes, something came up and I needed to see her.

Paula It's your fault.

Miranda It's my fault. Yes. I'm sorry. Very last moment. Yes, of course . . . absolutely the last time. I'll explain that, yes. (*She puts down the phone.*)

Paula Thanks. Are you moving?

Miranda It's my other half. He's moving out.

Paula Oh, sorry.

Miranda He'll probably want to come back soon. He's not a strong character.

Paula I can't imagine you with someone weak.

Miranda It was a mistake.

Paula I can't imagine you making a mistake.

Miranda I just hate seeing his things around. It's like being punched all the time. Well, you know what it's like. Getting someone out of your life.

Paula Smash something up.

Miranda Is that what you do?

Paula It helps.

Miranda You mean something like this. (*Pulls a disk out of a box.*) His book.

Paula Is it important?

Miranda He's been working on it for ten years.

Paula That'll do.

Miranda He'll have copies.

Paula It's symbolic, isn't it?

Miranda puts it aside. Picks up a lone trainer.

Miranda I don't know what to do with this. It's just the one.

Paula Chuck it away.

Miranda You see, if I'm not careful, Paula, this is what's going to happen to me.

Paula What is?

Miranda Packed away. People would like to pack me away. They've tried to shrink me and that's because they want to make me scared to ask for things.

Paula Who?

Miranda But I'm not going to start thinking small. I'm going to start thinking bigger than ever.

Paula Oh.

Miranda Imagine, Paula. That you could be anything,

anyone you wanted to be. Who would you be? What would you be? Imagine, Paula. Go on. Now.

Paula What?

Miranda Anything. Anything. Just imagine. (*Pause.*) All right. A scientist. I can see you as a scientist working with a team on a cure for leukaemia. You could help so many people. Children. Think of the gratitude of their parents. If you think about the human body, Paula, it's an incredible thing. The arteries, the veins reach into every part of us. And the blood itself breaks down into individual cells and each cell is a beautifully functioning system. And each of us has countless millions of them inside us. Perfect structures. Can you see yourself like that? That's how big we need think. That big.

Pause.

Paula So didn't Emma have any luck? The picture?

Miranda She didn't have immediate luck. But I know she could, Paula. If she wanted to keep trying. I've got a conviction about that.

Paula I better get back.

Miranda I'll see you next week, Paula. Same time as usual.

Paula leaves.
Miranda treads on Roger's disk. Stands looking at the pieces.

SCENE SIX

The Hooded Man and Emma. Hooded Man hands Emma a cup of tea.

Hooded Man White, no sugar.

Emma Thanks.

Hooded Man I thought you seemed a bit different today.

Emma Different?

Hooded Man More sad, less angry.

Emma I almost killed someone the other day.

Hooded Man My God. Did you get carried away?

Emma He nearly did. In an ambulance. We thought it was his heart.

Hooded Man They do say it's important to eat a lot of fruit.

Emma It's just another thing to think about.

Hooded Man Tell me if I'm invading your privacy.

Emma All right.

Hooded Man So what do you do? For a living?

Emma I'm a failed artist.

Hooded Man Really?

Emma Yes.

Hooded Man Sketching?

Emma Sketching is involved.

Hooded Man Could you draw me?

Emma I can draw anything that sits still for long enough

Hooded Man Draw me.

Emma Can you supply the paper?

The Hooded Man opens his briefcase and takes out pe
and paper. Gives them to Emma.

Emma Well equipped as always.

Hooded Man That's what my wife always says.

Emma Aren't you going to take off the hood?

Hooded Man No, no. I want the hood.

Emma Please yourself.

Hooded Man Art's a hobby of mine, funnily enough.

They sit while she sketches.

Emma Talk to me.

Hooded Man What about?

Emma Why do you always wear a hood?

Hooded Man I enjoy it immensely.

Emma Why?

Hooded Man I just do.

Emma Can't you do better than that?

Hooded Man For you I can.

Emma Good. That's what I like to hear.

Hooded Man I like its darkness. I like being inside. Completely inside. Total enclosure. Nothing getting in. My own private world. Only children normally have that privilege. Is that satisfactory?

Emma It'll do. There.

Hooded Man That really is rather choice.

Emma Oh, thanks.

Hooded Man Can I have it?

Emma If you want.

Hooded Man How much?

Emma Oh, no. Really. You can keep it.

Hooded Man That is silly. Throwing yourself away like that. How much?

Emma You really want it?

Hooded Man Yes.

Emma What would you do if I tore it up?

Hooded Man I'd be most upset.

Emma Say, 'Please, Emma, don't tear it.'

Hooded Man Please, Emma, don't tear it.

Emma 'It's very precious.'

Hooded Man It's very precious.

Emma A hundred pounds.

Hooded Man Seventy-five.

Emma Done.

Hooded Man I know a lot of people. Only it's not an interpretive field. Just drawing what's there.

Emma I prefer that. Just what's there.

Hooded Man Do you work in any other materials?

SCENE SEVEN

The group room. Nicola follows Miranda in.

Nicola I was nervous. I did OK, I think. I answered all the questions.

Miranda Well done.

Nicola Thanks. God knows what I'll face when I get home. The end of the world probably. That's what he was predicting when I left. Still, I've done it now. I've done it. I can't believe it.

Miranda Yes, congratulations.

Nicola I could never have got through it without you.

Miranda It was your hard work.

Nicola I wanted to say thank you.

Miranda You've no need to.

Nicola Paula's outside. She's just finishing her cigarette.

Miranda Emma won't be coming.

Pause.

Nicola I do think 'poor Dad'. He's sort of stuck, isn't he? And I'm moving away from him. I'll leave him. I will come back and visit, but it's not the same, is it? He'll be alone. I always say to myself the things you told me. I'm not just there to take care of him. I have rights too. I'm a person. He always rows with me about what I'm doing. Psychology, sociology. Passports to inconsequentiality. But then the other day I told him. I know what I want to do. I want to do what Miranda does. What you do.

Paula enters. She launches in.

Paula This is what happened. I'm not proud. I saw Victoria last Wednesday week, didn't we, Nick? Anyway, Tuesday I get a letter. I thought, this is fucking ridiculous, my own daughter writing me a letter. 'I've got my passport photos done on Saturday.' Passport photos! I went to work, then something went snap in my mind. I took twenty quid from the till and told them to fucking forget it. I got the train down, then I take a cab to Victoria's school. March into her classroom. I can hear the teacher asking me things. I just take Victoria. We go to the station. Next thing the police come. They take Victoria off me. I shout. I swear at them. They put me in a car. I resist. I fall over getting pushed into the car. That's how I got my eye. (*She turns slightly to show her eye, which is bruised.*) On the bright side, there's no charges because everyone's being understanding and I won't be working nights because now I won't be working. How bad is it? How badly have I fucked up?

Miranda I don't think the group is the place to discuss it, do you?

Paula Nick doesn't mind.

Miranda Whether she minds or not isn't the point.

Paula What is the point?

Miranda We need to discuss it on a one-to-one basis.

Paula Just tell me. (*Pause.*) I lost my head. I didn't hurt anyone.

Miranda And the eye?

Paula Yes?

Miranda Your eye.

Paula My eye? Yes?

Miranda You knocked it?

Paula Getting into the car. Yes?

Miranda I have to be satisfied, totally satisfied that you can provide a safe home for your daughter.

Paula Yes?

Miranda Yes.

Paula So this is a question about Michael? (*Pause.*) So I've seen him again. It's not against the law just because you've got some idea in your head. I fell getting into the car.

Miranda I don't believe you.

Paula This is rubbish. Are you telling me who I can screw? I actually like to screw. I'm not Mother Teresa. What is it? Do you want to choose someone for me? In your partnership role? I know you'll go for the GCSEs but can I put in a plea for a nice cock?

Miranda It's a clear issue.

Paula It's not a clear issue though, is it? He's never touched Victoria. Only me. Sometimes. And other people, not you, might decide that that is not adequate reason to keep a child from her mother.

Miranda So it's acceptable for her to watch you being beaten.

Nicola Please don't fight.

Miranda You have to make a choice. Michael or Victoria.

Paula I don't have to choose.

Miranda Not choosing is choosing Michael.

Paula I tell you something, Miranda. What I have chosen. I've chosen not to have you. I don't want to see you. I don't want to talk to you. I want someone else. Someone more reasonable. More normal. With less hang-ups. Someone who'll see my side.

Miranda Do you think you'll find someone who's prepared to give you what you want, no questions asked? A different sort of social worker? That's not going to happen, Paula, you might as well wake up to that. Choose your daughter.

Paula I'm not letting you choose for me. Imagine a future, any future, as long as it's the same as yours, Miranda. I'd rather swallow poison.

Miranda What are you going to do, Paula? Go back to your shitty life? Prostituting yourself. Living with a bastard. Just existing from day to day, barely coping. You ought to be glad that I was prepared to take you on.

Paula You're a fucking disaster for me.

Nicola Please stop arguing. Please.

Paula The thing is, sometimes I ask him to hit me. I ask him because I prefer pain on the outside. I prefer it.

Miranda I think you're very confused.

Paula No.

Miranda You're a mess, Paula. A mess!

Paula gets out her razor. She makes a cut in her arm.

Nicola Don't, Paula.

Miranda Don't do that, Paula.

Paula I prefer this. I prefer it on the outside. That's better. That's much, much better.

Nicola You're bleeding.

Paula It's just a cut.

Nicola She's bleeding.

Miranda Let me get something for your arm, Paula.

Paula No. I've got something in my bag. You get it, Nick.

Nicola gets Paula's bag.

Cloth.

Nicola hands Paula a cloth, which she holds against her arm.

You don't know me. What I feel. You imagine you do, Miranda, but you don't. You go home to your nice house and your nice money. You don't know what it's like in the real world.

Miranda I do know. I told people I'd been sick. That was the easiest thing to say. But to tell the truth I was exhausted in a different sort of way. (*Pause.*) I found a child. Quite a young child. It was dead. Starved actually. A bus ride from here. A neighbour let me in. I really couldn't believe what I was seeing. I mean, you hear about things. You read reports, but it doesn't prepare you. I remember standing in that room and just feeling my mind emptying. Till there was nothing. Just me and the child in the room. When I got closer to the child I saw there were little cuts on its body. Tiny cuts. Hundreds of tiny cuts. Like stitches, but cuts. You only take that much care if it affords you some satisfaction. You see, I can understand anger, I can forgive anger. But satisfaction? Isn't that pleasure? It took me a long time, a long time to get back to myself after that.

Nicola That's like a sign. Dad would say it was a sign.

Miranda No, no. It's not a sign.

Nicola What is it then?

Miranda What pulled me through was the thought that I was needed. Because if people stopped caring . . . (*She gathers up her stuff.*) I'm tired.

Nicola Where are you going?

Miranda I'm tired.

Nicola You can't go. I need to talk to you.

Miranda Talk to Paula. (*She exits.*)

Nicola She's gone. I always felt safe here.

Paula You don't need her, Nick. Better off without her. You can get on with your own life. (*She lights up.*)

Nicola And water will fall from the sky. Floods will bury us, darkness will come and God's light will fade from the world.

Paula watches her, a bit alarmed.

That's Dad. Not me.

Paula Oh. You had me going there a minute. I'll be back here Monday. Starting all over a-fucking-gain. You'll be all right though, Nick. Students. They have a brilliant time. All they do is drink and have sex and then when their exams come up they take lots of pills to stay awake and do the studying they've been too busy to do before. Fantastic.

Nicola You have to study hard nowadays. There's a lot of competition for jobs. And you have to work too. Because you can't live off your grant.

Paula Oh. Oh well. Good luck.

Nicola Yes. I suppose I will go.

Paula Course you'll go. You can't stay with your old man, he's a lunatic.

Nicola What am I going for though?

Paula Well, it's something to do, isn't it? You can get a job at the end of it.

Nicola I didn't just want a job. I wanted something. Something I wanted to do. I wanted to feel something. That I was doing something important. Special. I didn't just want to join up dots. A to B. With no feeling behind it. Do you know what I mean?

Paula I don't know. I've got a headache. You'll be all right, Nick. You'll be fine. You'll study. You'll be brilliant. Then you'll land some dossy job.

Nicola But I want something. Something.

Paula Like me. I want Michael and Victoria and a bit of money. Look at the fucking time. I'm meeting Michael. Fancy a drink?

Nicola No, no. I better get back.

Paula Another time, Nick. Keep in touch.

Nicola Yes. Yes. I'll turn the lights out.

Paula You'll be fucking brilliant, Nick. Honestly.

Paula exits. Nicola stands for a moment looking at the room. There is a bright flash of light, noise. Whether it is frightening, as in a thunderstorm, or hopeful, as in a bright future, is ambiguous. Nicky stands unsure.
Lights go down.